Endorsements

Barry Bennett's teachings have transformed and renewed our minds. With thousands of hours of teaching experience at Charis Bible School, Barry's ability to present God's promise of healing is clear and precise. Sit under Barry Bennett's gift in this book and your life will never be the same.

—John Tesh and Connie Sellecca

Barry Bennett is one of the premier teachers in the body of Christ today. I have known him for many years and every time I have heard him teach or read a book or article he has written, I have been enriched and encouraged by the revelation he imparts from the Word. This book, *He Healed Them All*, is one of the most complete books on the subject of healing I have read. Barry answers many questions people have about healing and I am confident that after reading this book, revelation will come to you and faith will rise in your heart to receive your healing!

—Greg Mohr
Director
Charis Bible College, Colorado

He
HEALED
Them ALL

Harrison
House

Shippensburg, PA

Harrison House Books by Barry Bennett

Did God Do This to Me?

Accessing God's Grace for Divine Health and Healing

He HEALED *Them* ALL

BARRY BENNETT

Dedication

To my loving wife, Betty Kay, and our three children, David, Daniel and Leah, and their families, who have all been a part of this journey into God's grace for health and healing.

Published by Harrison House Publishers
Shippensburg, PA 17257

Cover design by Eileen Rockwell

ISBN 13 TP: 978-1-6803-1412-0

ISBN 13 eBook: 978-1-6803-1418-2

ISBN 13 HC: 978-1-6803-1430-4

ISBN 13 LP: 978-1-6803-1429-8

For Worldwide Distribution, Printed in the U.S.A.

1 2 3 4 5 6 7 8 / 24 23 22 21 20

Contents

Foreword

Healing is something that affects every single person on this planet. In this fallen world, we all deal with sickness and the devastation it brings. People spend billions of dollars on treatments and billions more trying to prevent sickness. It's one of the biggest issues of life and the Lord has not left us to our own devices in this very important area.

Jesus purchased healing for our bodies just as much as He purchased the forgiveness of our sins. That's a radical statement to most people and that's one of the big reasons most people don't experience Divine healing. They just don't know the truth of what Jesus has done in this area.

Jesus said that the truth would set us free (John 8:32) but it's only the truth we know that sets us free. What people don't know about healing is literally killing them.

In this book Barry Bennett shares these basic truths about how to receive healing directly from God in such a practical way that you can't miss it. He also explains how to overcome many of the hinderances that keep people from receiving the healing that Jesus has already provided. This will answer many questions.

This isn't just theory with Barry. He has experienced miraculous healings himself and also in his family. He teaches a course on healing in our Charis Bible College and I don't believe it is an exaggeration to say thousands of people have also received their healing because of the truths Barry shares with them.

If you need healing or know someone who does or if you don't need healing at this moment, you will in the future and therefore, this book is for you. The best time to learn about healing isn't when the battle for health is raging. It's before the storm breaks and you can lay the foundation of healing in the calm before the storm.

I've known Barry and his family for years and he is consistent. He walks with the Lord and never fails to deliver fresh revelation directly from the throne. Barry is a humble man who exalts the Lord and not himself and therefore has great grace on his life (1 Peter 5:5-6). This relationship and the grace upon him provide a channel for the Lord to flow through that will enrich your life. You need this book.

I believe the Lord is reaching out to you through this book. The Lord has anointed Barry to share these truths in such a simple, practical way that you will never be the same. Get ready to receive your healing and let that miraculous healing power flow through you to others.

—**Andrew Wommack**

God's Heart for You Is Abundant Life

...I have come that they may have life, and that they may have it more abundantly (John 10:10).

There is grace for you to experience abundant life. Before you continue reading this book, I want you to know that Jesus cares for you and wants you well. Health and healing are His will for all men, women, and children on this planet. He has made provision for forgiveness and healing for all mankind. His provision is known as "grace" in the Bible. And there is enough for you.

> *And Jesus went forth, and saw a great multitude, and was moved with compassion toward them, and **he healed their sick** (Matthew 14:14 KJV).*

Jesus' compassion has not diminished. I can find no evidence in the gospels of Jesus ever questioning why someone was sick or assigning guilt to them. I can find no evidence of Jesus indicating that sickness had a divine purpose or that it was a blessing in disguise. I cannot find one example of Jesus saying "no" to anyone who sought Him for healing. He was full of compassion and healed the sick. He was full of grace and His grace is still alive today.

> ...*And great multitudes followed Him, and* **He healed them all** (Matthew 12:15).

God hates sickness! He hates its source and He hates its impact on human lives. It was not part of His creation and it is always referred to in negative terms in the Bible. Why have so many Christians found a positive place for sickness in their theology when Jesus so obviously waged warfare against it?

Much of Jesus' ministry revolved around healing the sick. It is noticeable that all who came to Him were healed. There is no case in Scripture in which Jesus denied healing to someone who came to Him, or said that the sick one was suffering according to God's divine purpose. He healed them all.

After Jesus' resurrection, in the early church in Acts chapter 5, we find the following:

> *Also a multitude gathered from the surrounding cities to Jerusalem, bringing sick people and those who were tormented by unclean spirits, and* **they were all healed** (Acts 5:16).

It wouldn't be wrong to say that if you needed healing and had been in the crowd that made its way to the church in Jerusalem, you would have been healed. Healing was for all in Jesus' ministry and it was for all in the early church. Has anything changed?

Allow hope to be born in your heart. The grace of God is bigger than any affliction or sickness you may be experiencing. Read and meditate on each truth presented in these pages. Believe that His Word is at work in you to set you free and heal you.

Chapter 1

Is Healing for Today?

It was 1989, and my wife and I and our three children were living in Huehuetenango, Guatemala, to study Spanish. We arrived in Guatemala in January and would be transitioning to a ministry in Chile in November.

At some point in September, we made a trip to a mountain village to share the gospel. We were invited to eat a meal while there and the environment was very rustic. A few days after that trip I began to feel sick and weak. This lasted several days until finally one morning I looked in the mirror and noticed my eyeballs were yellow! I went to my wife and asked if she noticed anything, and she immediately said, "Oh Barry, you have hepatitis!"

I went to a local doctor who ran some blood tests and confirmed that I had a very serious case and that I would need to be in bed on a strict diet for four months. I didn't have four months left in the country, so I was not happy.

A missionary friend stopped by with a box of books and tapes about faith and healing for me to study. I was already a believer in healing and could teach the principles of healing to some extent. I didn't need to be convinced, but I did need to be healed.

I spent hours a day for the next four weeks reading, listening to tapes, and praying. One day while my family was at the market, I shuffled out of my bedroom "quarantine" and sat down in our kitchen area. I was praying and meditating on all I had been studying, and suddenly I "heard" God say to me, "Barry, by My stripes you were healed." I knew that, but suddenly I KNEW it! God had spoken to me in a similar way several years earlier and had given me a revelation of righteousness. This was now the second time that a revelation of truth changed me.

A REVELATION OF TRUTH

Suddenly I knew I was healed! There was not a doubt in my mind or heart. I asked myself, *What would a healed person do right now?* I got up, got dressed, and left the house for the first time in four weeks, and I took a walk up and down the street. I had lost a lot of weight and I was still yellow, but I was healed. I went back to a normal diet, normal activities, and never looked back. I have never had a liver problem since.

Whether or not my body would have recovered naturally over time isn't really the point of this story. The real point is that we can hear God and that healing is an accomplished part of our redemption. In God's eyes, I was always healed. It just took me four weeks to believe it. The sooner we see it and believe it, the sooner sickness will lose its grip on our lives.

Some would say that healing passed away with the last of the apostles or healing passed away when the New Testament Scriptures were completed. Many won't deny that God can heal if He wants to, but they believe healing isn't something that we can count on. They view healing as one of the mysteries of God and that some are healed but many are not.

Have healing and the other gifts of the Spirit passed away? Let's look at some reasons that confirm that the gifts of the Spirit and healing remain alive in the church today.

> *And He [Jesus] said to them, "Go into all the world and preach the gospel to every creature. He who believes and is baptized will be saved; but he who does not believe will be condemned. And these signs will follow those who believe: In My name they will cast out demons; they will speak with new tongues; they will take up serpents; and if they drink anything deadly, it will by no means hurt them; they will lay hands on the sick, and they will recover"* (Mark 16:15-18).

In Mark 16:15-18, the command to the disciples and by extension to the church, is to go into all the world and preach the gospel. We can see that this command is not just for the original apostles of the Lord since it was physically impossible for them to accomplish this commission within their lifetimes. Not only were they limited by the length of their earthly lives, they were limited by the lack of available transportation to reach every tribe and nation on earth. Either the gospel is for every nation and every human or it isn't.

TO ALL WHO BELIEVE

Jesus' commission wasn't just to the apostles therefore, but to the entire church. If not, then we are not called to preach the gospel today because that commission died with the last apostle. This is a serious point. Are we or are we not called to reach the nations with the gospel? Was this command only to the apostles of the Lord? If the command is viable and active for us today, then what follows is also pertinent.

In Mark 16:16, Jesus said, *"He who believes,"* which refers to those of the nations who become believers at the preaching of the gospel. In verse 17, He continues, *"And these signs will follow those who believe."* This is a promise to those same new believers. The new believers of verse 16 are the same believers who have signs following them in verse 17.

What signs will follow these new believers? They shall cast out demons, they shall speak with new tongues, they shall take up serpents—as in the case of Paul on the island, when one bit him and he suffered no harm (Acts 28:3-6)—if they drink any deadly thing, it shall not hurt them, and they shall lay hands on the sick and they shall recover.

When the disciples received this commission, Mark continues: *"And they went out and preached everywhere, the Lord working with them and confirming the word through the accompanying signs"* (Mark 16:20).

The Lord was working with them, confirming the Word with signs. The Lord is still working with those who believe and still confirms the Word with signs—healings and miracles—following.

If the preaching of the gospel is meant for all nations, then the signs that follow that preaching are still valid. And those who respond to that preaching will also have signs follow. Logic dictates that the apostles of the Lord couldn't be around generation after generation to lay hands on each new believer for them to receive the power of the Spirit. The power wasn't the apostle's power, it is the Lord's power and confirms the gospel. It still does.

THE FATHER'S PROMISE

Let us now consider the promise of the Father that was received by the 120 on the day of Pentecost and was preached by Peter on that same day. The *"gift of the Holy Spirit"* was announced as being for *"as many as the Lord our God shall call"* (Acts 2:38-39).

> *Then Peter said to them, "Repent, and let every one of you be baptized in the name of Jesus Christ for the remission of sins; and you shall receive the gift of the Holy Spirit. For the promise is to you and to your children, and to all who are afar off, as many as the Lord our God will call (Acts 2:38-39).*

There is no expiration date on this promise! The gift of the Holy Spirit is promised to all whom the Lord calls—and He has called all! He is *"not willing that any should perish"*! (See 2 Peter 3:9.)

> *Behold, I send the Promise of My Father upon you; but tarry in the city of Jerusalem until you are endued with power from on high (Luke 24:49).*

And being assembled together with them, Jesus commanded them not to depart from Jerusalem, but to wait for the Promise of the Father, *"'which,' He said, 'you have heard from Me'"* (Acts 1:4).

Why would the disciples need to be endued with power?

> *But you shall receive power when the Holy Spirit*
> *has come upon you; and you shall be witnesses to*
> *Me in Jerusalem, and in all Judea and Samaria,*
> *and to the end of the earth* (Acts 1:8).

The power was in order to be a witness of the Lord to the end of the earth! Again, the original apostles were not going to finish the job of reaching the ends of the earth. But I believe most would agree that reaching the lost is still the heart of God. Are we to reach the lost and be witnesses with power or with no power? If the commission to go into all the world remains valid, the power to accomplish God's will must remain valid as well.

THE GIFTS OF THE SPIRIT

Now, let's consider God's plan concerning the gifts of the Spirit.

> *For the gifts and the calling of God are irrevocable*
> (Romans 11:29).

The Greek word for gifts is *charisma* and is the same word used to refer to the gifts of the Spirit described in 1 Corinthians, chapter 12.

There are diversities of gifts, but the same Spirit (1 Corinthians 12:4).

Paul declares that the gifts, *charisma,* of God are irrevocable and there are a diversity of *charisma.* What does irrevocable mean?

The Greek word for irrevocable is *ametameletos,* meaning not to be repented of. In other words, God will not change His mind about the role of the Holy Spirit in the affairs of mankind and in the preaching of the gospel to the nations.

These irrevocable, *charisma* gifts are described in 1 Corinthians 12:

> *For to one is given the word of wisdom through the Spirit, to another the word of knowledge through the same Spirit, to another faith by the same Spirit, to another gifts of healings by the same Spirit, to another the working of miracles, to another prophecy, to another discerning of spirits, to another different kinds of tongues, to another the interpretation of tongues* (1 Corinthians 12:8-10).

These gifts are the *charisma* that are irrevocable and follow the preaching of the gospel. These gifts are part of the great commission to reach all nations. Healing is part of the gospel message to all people.

Thus far we have the witness of three: 1)The Great Commission to all nations with signs following; 2) the Promise of the Father of the Baptism of the Holy Spirit (endued with power from on high, choose your favorite term), which is for all who come to the Lord; and 3) the gifts of God that are irrevocable.

We can add to that Paul's clear statement in 1 Corinthians chapter 1: *"So that you come short in no gift, eagerly waiting for the revelation of our Lord Jesus Christ"* (1 Corinthians 1:7).

The word "gift" is once again the Greek word *charisma*. Paul's understanding was that the gifts of the Spirit would be in operation until the coming of the Lord. We can confirm this with the famous quote of Jesus in Acts 1:8:

> *But you shall receive power when the Holy Spirit has come upon you; and you shall be witnesses to Me in Jerusalem, and in all Judea and Samaria, and to the end of the earth.*

This promise is for the power that we need to reach the nations with the gospel of God's love. Until that commission is completed, the power is here and available to those who believe.

Jesus declared:

> *And this gospel of the kingdom will be preached in all the world as a witness to all the nations, and then the end will come* (Matthew 24:14).

Once this gospel is preached to all the world as a witness (Acts 1:8), then the power, the signs, the tongues, and other gifts will have fulfilled their purpose. There will be no more need. But as long as the Great Commission is in effect, the power, the gifts, and the signs are irrevocable.

HEALING IS AVAILABLE TODAY

Healing is available today. It is available to you. As we open our hearts to the truths of God's Word, it will awaken our hope and build our faith to expect healing. Jesus is the same yesterday, today, and forever (Hebrews 13:8). It is not reasonable to suggest that Jesus would heal all who came to Him, and that all who came to the first church in Jerusalem were healed, but now God's attitude toward human suffering has somehow changed. If you had lived 2,000 years ago and had sought out Jesus, or had made your way to the first church, you would have been healed. Why not now? Could it be that our expectations are too low?

Healing should be as expected today as it was in the gospels and the book of Acts. It is my intention to bring some much-needed light to the subject and encourage your heart to *hear Him and be healed* (Luke 5:15).

HEALING PRAYER

Father, open my heart to truly hear Your Word and know Your heart for my life. I agree with Your promise of abundant life! Amen!

Chapter 2

The Message of the Kingdom

Jesus never taught healing. He preached the Kingdom and demonstrated the Kingdom. Healing is a benefit of the Kingdom.

> *But when the multitudes knew it, they followed Him; and **He received them** and spoke to them about the kingdom of God, **and healed those who had need of healing*** (Luke 9:11).

The gospel of the Kingdom was an introduction into the meaning of redemption. Freedom from guilt and condemnation, forgiveness of sin, and physical healing are all included in the gospel message. Faith in the finished work of the cross is the door into Kingdom living.

We cannot separate healing from forgiveness. Jesus didn't. A paralytic man was carried to Jesus on a stretcher by four friends. When they were unable to get into the house where Jesus was ministering, they climbed up to the roof and pulled the tiles away, making a hole through which the paralytic was lowered. Obviously, Jesus had to stop His message and address the distraction.

When Jesus saw their faith, He said to the paralytic, *"Son, your sins are forgiven you"* (Mark 2:5).

Put yourself in the place of the paralyzed man. He had come from some distance being carried on a stretcher. He had been jostled through a crowd, carried up to a roof and then let down on ropes through a hole in the roof. Undoubtedly, he was expecting something, but I don't think he was expecting what Jesus said! *"Your sins are forgiven you."* What?

It is very important that we consider this statement because it reveals a powerful truth concerning the condition of mankind and the redemption that Jesus came to give us. After a debate with the religious leaders who were offended by Jesus declaring that a man's sins were forgiven, Jesus continued with a challenge.

> *Which is easier, to say to the paralytic, "Your sins are forgiven you," or to say, "Arise, take up your bed and walk"?* (Mark 2:9)

In our day it is certainly easier to speak of the forgiveness of sin because that is invisible to the natural eye. Healing is very visible. But are they connected? We will study this more in coming chapters but let's follow the story of the paralytic.

> *"But that you may know that the Son of Man has power on earth to forgive sins"*—He said to the paralytic, *"I say to you, arise, take up your bed, and go to your house." Immediately he arose, took up the bed, and went out in the presence of them all,*

*so that all were amazed and glorified God, saying,
"We never saw anything like this!"* (Mark 2:10-12)

In the mind and heart of Jesus, forgiveness and healing were interconnected. In fact, the forgiveness of sin was the key that unlocked the healing. Both forgiveness and healing speak of salvation. One is invisible and the other quite visible. Sickness is a result of sin in the earth. If sin has been forgiven, the power of sickness has been defeated! If we deal with the root, which is sin, we've dealt with the fruit, which is sickness.

THE ROOT IS SIN—THE FRUIT IS SICKNESS

What about the multitudes of people Jesus healed during His years of ministry? Does this mean that He was forgiving their sins as well?

Therefore let it be known to you, brethren, that through this Man is preached to you the forgiveness of sins (Acts 13:38).

Jesus was preaching and demonstrating the Kingdom. If healing was taking place, it is because forgiveness was taking place. Grace was taking place! Jesus was demonstrating the Kingdom of God. That grace causes some to stumble and doubt, but I believe the Scriptures are clear that God's grace for humanity includes forgiveness and healing for whosoever will.

> *That is, that God was in Christ reconciling the world to Himself, not imputing their trespasses to them...* (2 Corinthians 5:19).

In this age of grace, sin is not being imputed. This means that God is not judging sin. Sin carries its own consequences; but those are consequences, not divine judgment. *Sickness is not the judgment of God! Forgiveness and healing are the grace of God!*

This is why the disciples were commissioned to go into all the world, preach the gospel, and heal the sick. This is what Jesus was demonstrating when He healed the paralytic. The power of sickness and death is sin, Adam's sin. If Jesus forgives sin, sickness has no foundation on which to stand. If we truly understood this, healing would be released into our bodies.

God's will has always been health and healing for men and women whom He created in His image. If we are going to understand healing, we must understand God's heart.

> *Then God saw everything that He had made, and indeed it was very good...* (Genesis 1:31).

In the beginning, God's creation was very good. It was perfect. There was no death, no sickness, no loss, and no suffering. Adam and Eve were at peace with God and living in a world of perfection. What happened?

> *Therefore, just as through one man sin entered the world, and death through sin...* (Romans 5:12).

Adam's sin unleashed the power of death. Sin in its most simple definition is "independence from God." Adam and Eve could have chosen to be dependent on God and His words, or they could become independent and listen to the voice of the serpent. Their choice of independence unleased the consequence of separation—death. Death, corruption, and Satan's rule in the earth were unleashed by one act of independence from God and His Word.

Sickness is simply death in its first stages. All sicknesses have but one purpose—to steal, kill, and destroy. Sickness hastens death. A death due to sickness is always premature. Sickness steals time and thwarts our divine purpose in this world. Sickness destroys the quality of life. It steals resources and destroys futures. Sickness is a horrible consequence of sin in the human race. Sickness was not part of God's creation.

We can understand God's attitude toward sickness by considering Jesus' words and actions:

> *For I have come down from heaven, not to do My own will, but the will of Him who sent Me* (John 6:38).

From this declaration we can understand that Jesus' ministry was a direct revelation of the Father's heart for humanity. What Jesus did on earth was a manifestation of the Father's nature and will.

> *God anointed **Jesus** of Nazareth with the Holy Spirit and with power, who **went about doing good and healing all** who were oppressed by the devil, for God was with Him* (Acts 10:38).

Please note that doing the will of Him who sent Jesus included *"doing good and healing all."* Why? Because God was with Him. In other words, where God is and where His will is being done, healing takes place. It is clear that where God's presence is, healing should be taking place.

> *Now a leper came to Him, imploring Him, kneeling down to Him and saying to Him, "If You are willing, You can make me clean." Then Jesus, moved with compassion, stretched out His hand and touched him, and said to him, "I am willing; be cleansed"* (Mark 1:40-41).

This is the only case we have in the gospels of someone asking Jesus if it was His will to heal. His response should satisfy us that if it was His will for this leper, it is His will for all. God does not value one suffering life above another. Jesus didn't question why this man might have leprosy. He didn't question his heart, mention any sin, or explain that the Father was teaching him something. Jesus was simply moved with compassion and healed him. He was willing. Why? Because He was doing the Father's will.

This type of scene is repeated throughout the gospels. Jesus healed all who came to Him. He healed them all!

> *Jesus Christ is the same yesterday, today, and forever* (Hebrews 13:8).

Some would declare that Jesus no longer heals today, or only heals if He wants to in special circumstances. However, I doubt any would question His forgiveness for all who believe. Why would we take a stand for the ongoing redemptive work of forgiveness, but limit healing to a special category of uncertainty?

YES AND AMEN

In Mark chapter 5 we find the story of Jairus. He implored Jesus to come to His house and heal his daughter. Jesus went with him. He didn't ask questions. He was about His Father's business, and the Father sent Jesus to heal.

As Jesus made His way to the house of Jairus, He was approached from behind by a woman who had suffered from a hemorrhage for twelve years. Knowing that she was considered unclean according to the Law of Moses, she nevertheless made her way through the crowd and came up behind Jesus without His knowledge. She simply touched the hem of His garment and was instantly healed. How? Jesus didn't even know who had touched Him. There was no time for a healing interview. There was no time to discern if she was worthy, if she was in sin, or if she was being "chastised" by God for her own good.

She simply believed that she would be healed; and when she touched Jesus' garment, she was healed. Why? When it comes to faith, Jesus is always yes and amen. The woman took what was being offered. Anyone could. Healing is always yes and amen! There was grace for her.

> *For all the promises of God in Him are Yes, and in Him Amen, to the glory of God through us* (2 Corinthians 1:20).

Healing is a promise for whosoever will. Sadly, many Christians struggle with this concept and hinder God's will in their lives.

The miracle of the woman with the issue of blood gave birth to a movement!

> *Wherever He entered into villages, cities, or in the country, they laid the sick in the marketplaces, and begged Him that they might just touch the hem of His garment. And as many as touched Him were made well* (Mark 6:56).

When the Good News of the nature and power of God gets out, hope is born and faith is conceived. This same Good News has not lost its power today. Healing is part of the Kingdom message.

If healing isn't for all, how can it be for any? The very fact that our bodies are designed to fight sickness and heal themselves is testimony to the fact that God wants us well. Strong, healthy bodies can resist or defeat most sicknesses. When we abuse our bodies or suffer from emotional or physical trauma or we live in fear and stress, our bodies weaken and sicknesses seek an opportunity against us. Nevertheless, healing is available to all just as salvation from sin is available to all.

As we continue through this book, I hope to convince you that healing is part of our redemption in Christ. We know that Jesus came to destroy the works of the enemy, and that He went about doing good and healing *all* who were oppressed of the devil, for God was with Him.

Just because there are still sinners on earth doesn't mean that Jesus failed in His mission to break the power of sin on the cross. Just because there are still sicknesses in the world doesn't mean that Jesus failed to defeat that curse as well.

> *...For this purpose the Son of God was manifested, that He might destroy the works of the devil* (1 John 3:8).

> *How God anointed Jesus of Nazareth with the Holy Spirit and with power, who went about doing good and healing all who were oppressed by the devil, for God was with Him* (Acts 10:38).

The works of the devil in 1 John 3:8 are linked to sicknesses in Acts 10:38. I don't believe that Jesus failed in His mission.

The problem isn't whether healing is God's will or not. The problem is often our lack of understanding of God's will. God stated, *"My people are destroyed for lack of knowledge"* (Hosea 4:6).

Our redemption was accomplished two thousand years ago and all of the benefits of that redemption became available at that time for all who believe. We have been freed from the power of sin and all its manifestations, including sickness.

We can find God's heart to see His people healed in many Scriptures in both Old and New Testaments. God reveals Himself in one of His redemptive names as the God who heals us— Jehovah Rapha.

> *...For I am the Lord who heals you* (Exodus 15:26).

God's nature cannot change, so if He was a healer before the Law of Moses and during the Law of Moses, how much more under the grace of our new covenant in Jesus? Our covenant is a better covenant, not a worse one. The promises of the New Covenant are better, not worse.

> *But now He has obtained a more excellent ministry, inasmuch as He is also Mediator of a better covenant, which was established on better promises* (Hebrews 8:6).

SPIRITUAL AND PHYSICAL HEALING

Some might say that the healing available after the apostles passed away is only "spiritual healing." I have never understood that term, but let's give it some thought. Apart from the obvious focus of Jesus on physical healing, we also have the great commission with signs following. We have the charisma gifts of the Spirit that include healing, which we are not to neglect until the coming of the Lord (1 Corinthians 1:7).

We also have the exhortation of James that the prayer of faith would save the sick and the Lord would raise them up (James 5:14-16). And we have the incredible example of multitudes of sick people coming to Jerusalem and all are healed (Acts 5:16). In all of these cases the healing is physical. Why would it be different for believers today?

If healing today is only spiritual, what is the spiritual sickness? When we are born again, we are made complete in Him.

And you are complete in Him, who is the head of all principality and power (Colossians 2:10).

What part of us is complete? Our spirit is complete.

Therefore, if anyone is in Christ, he is a new creation; old things have passed away; behold, all things have become new (2 Corinthians 5:17).

What things have become new? Our spirit has become new.

For He made Him who knew no sin to be sin for us, that we might become the righteousness of God in Him (2 Corinthians 5:21).

What part of us has become righteous? Our spirit has been made complete, new, and righteous!

We must understand these incredible declarations are the description of our new and reborn spirit.

And that you put on the new man which was created according to God, in true righteousness and holiness (Ephesians 4:24).

If our spirit is complete, new, righteous, and holy, in what sense can it need healing? Wouldn't healing be necessary for our souls and bodies, not for our re-created spirits? Are we not one with Him?

But he who is joined to the Lord is one spirit with Him (1 Corinthians 6:17).

It is crucial that we understand the new creation and our reborn spirits if we are going to understand the New Covenant. Rather than looking for excuses to deny God's heart for our physical healing, we should be embracing His will for our lives that we might finish our course with strength!

Isaiah prophesied and Peter confirmed that by Jesus' stripes we were healed:

> *Surely He has borne our griefs and carried our sorrows; yet we esteemed Him stricken, smitten by God, and afflicted. But He was wounded for our transgressions, He was bruised for our iniquities; the chastisement for our peace was upon Him, and* **by His stripes we are healed** (Isaiah 53:4-5).

> *Who Himself bore our sins in His own body on the tree, that we, having died to sins, might live for righteousness—***by whose stripes you were healed** (1 Peter 2:24).

In other words, forgiveness exists for all people whether they receive it or not. The price was paid on the cross. Therefore, healing is also available to all, though many do not take advantage of it. Healing is just as available to the sick as forgiveness is to the sinner.

Jesus commissioned the church to heal the sick and we see the early church walking in this power. Jesus gave gifts of healing to the church and healing was expected.

James asked if any among the church is sick:

> *Is anyone among you sick? Let him call for the elders of the church, and let them pray over him, anointing him with oil in the name of the Lord* (James 5:14).

The very question implies that there should be no sick among us, and James gave the necessary steps to receive healing.

We need to stir ourselves up to resist the work of the enemy in our bodies. Just as we appropriate His grace to walk in holiness, let's appropriate His grace to walk in health. The gospel of the Kingdom is the gospel of healing for the whole person.

HEALING PRAYER

Father, I open my heart to the revelation of redemption in life. My spirit is new and one with You, and I receive the full blessing of healing in Jesus' name! Amen!

Chapter 3

Is Sickness a Blessing in Disguise?

I often hear sincere Christians describing their affliction as being the will of God for some greater good. Many times sickness is likened to a blessing or part of God's mysterious will. When we base our beliefs on supposed mysteries and not on the revealed Word of God, we are unwittingly cooperating with the corruption in the world and the power of the enemy to steal, kill, and destroy (John 10:10).

How does God describe sickness in the Bible? When we go to the Scriptures to see God's view of sickness, we come away with a different understanding than what is taught in many churches today. Sadly, many are taught that God uses sickness for our good. Some declare that He teaches us, perfects us, and keeps us humble by means of disease.

This begs the questions: If sickness, tragedy, and loss are our teachers, why did God give us His Word and His Spirit? Are they not meant to teach and perfect us?

All Scripture is given by inspiration of God, and is profitable for doctrine, for reproof, for correction, for instruction in righteousness, that the man of God may be complete, thoroughly equipped for every good work (2 Timothy 3:16-17).

Sickness, loss, tragedy, heartache, and destruction are not listed as being profitable that we may be equipped for every good work. Read it again. Those experiences are not listed. Our instruction in righteousness is not accomplished through sickness.

But the Helper, the Holy Spirit, whom the Father will send in My name, He will teach you all things... (John 14:26).

Is sickness a teacher that God has sent? Are the Word and the Spirit inadequate teachers for your life? Why isn't sickness mentioned as one of our teachers in the New Covenant? When believers adopt the idea that God teaches us through sickness, tragedy, loss and failure, they are actually declaring that they have no need for the Holy Spirit or the Bible, or that the Word and the Spirit are inadequate to accomplish God's will in our lives.

There is a religious mindset that unknowingly has rejected the full revelation of redemption and has embraced a theology of behavior modification. Some see themselves as unworthy or incomplete and the only way to receive good from God is to suffer at His hand and call it "love." For this reason millions of sincere believers find themselves sick and confused.

Consider the following verses in which God speaks of sickness for the first time in Scripture.

> *If you diligently heed the voice of the Lord your God and do what is right in His sight, give ear to His commandments and keep all His statutes, I will put none of the diseases on you which I have brought on the Egyptians. For **I am the Lord who heals you*** (Exodus 15:26).

In this passage, God refers to the diseases of the Egyptians as being a result of not hearkening to His voice. His heart toward Israel is that they walk in His ways. Egypt refers symbolically to the bondage of slavery that Israel had endured for hundreds of years. Sickness was a manifestation of bondage, not freedom. God revealed His nature in the fact that He wanted His people well. He revealed His name as the One who heals.

JEHOVAH RAPHA

"*I am the Lord who heals you.*" The word "heal" is the Hebrew word *rapha*. We will discuss this word later, but suffice it to say that God's name has been revealed as the Lord who heals! His name is a reflection of His nature, of His will and His purpose for His people. Sickness does not reflect God's heart for mankind.

Let's consider another example of God's view of sickness.

> *Moreover He will bring back on you all the diseases of Egypt, of which you were afraid, and they shall*

> *cling to you. Also every sickness and every plague,*
> *which is not written in this Book of the Law, will*
> *the Lord bring upon you until you are destroyed*
> (Deuteronomy 28:60-61).

Deuteronomy 28 is a chapter that reveals in great detail the blessings of obedience and the results for disobedience to the law of God. Of course, New Covenant believers are not under the law for right standing with Him. Jesus became that curse for us (Galatians 3:13). Nevertheless, we can learn the nature of God's blessings and God's view of sickness in this chapter.

Deuteronomy 28, from verse 15 until the end of the chapter, describes curses that will fall on the disobedient. Every sickness and every plague are considered curses, not blessings. The diseases of Egypt—bondage and slavery—are called curses.

Even under the Law of Moses, sickness was not God's will and was portrayed as a curse, not a blessing. How unusual that under our better covenant of grace so many believers embrace sickness as one of God's loving ways to bring us to Himself or teach us something! It is time to have our minds renewed to the Truth that will set us free!

For some reason, I have never had a problem in believing that God was for me, not against me. I have never been tempted to see sickness as a blessing or an instrument of teaching to perfect me. I have always seen sickness as a thief. But I know many fine Christians who don't have this conviction. I will discuss the root of this mindset a little later.

Consider God's view of Job's afflictions:

And the Lord turned the captivity of Job, when he prayed for his friends... (Job 42:10 KJV).

Job had been afflicted with sore boils from head to foot by the hand of Satan. God referred to this as *"captivity."* Job was not blessed with sickness. He was tormented by the captivity of the affliction. His suffering was not called a blessing. Having his captivity turned referred to healing. We will consider the story of Job later in this book.

When Jesus began His ministry in Israel, He read from the prophet Isaiah and declared the following:

The Spirit of the Lord is upon Me, because He has anointed Me to preach the gospel to the poor; He has sent Me to heal the brokenhearted, to proclaim liberty to the captives and recovery of sight to the blind, to set at liberty those who are oppressed (Luke 4:18).

In this opening statement of Jesus' purpose and God's will, we can find God's heart for His people. Jesus' mission was to help the poor, heal the brokenhearted, preach deliverance to the captives, recovery of sight to the blind, and to set free the oppressed. In this statement of purpose, Jesus does not mention making people sick or using their sickness to teach them anything.

The fact that much of Jesus' ministry involved physical healing demonstrates that the poor, brokenhearted, captive, blind, and bruised included those suffering physically. Sickness is captivity. It causes brokenheartedness and oppression. It creates poverty. *Sickness is a curse, never a blessing.*

It is interesting that the nature of Satan, the enemy, and the nature of sickness are the same. In John 10:10 we read, *"The thief does not come except to steal, and to kill, and to destroy. I [Jesus] have come that they may have life, and that they may have it more abundantly."* Doesn't it make sense that the thief and his works—sickness—share the same purpose? Sickness is a thief that steals time, money, and purpose. Sickness will kill you if it can, and it certainly destroys lives, families, and futures.

JESUS IS THE ANSWER

If Jesus came as the answer to sin's corruption and Satan's crimes, wouldn't it be obvious that the abundant life mentioned in John 10:10 would demonstrate the opposite of the works of the thief? Wouldn't abundant life include health and healing? I believe that yes, it would.

In Luke 13, we have the story of a poor woman doubled over for eighteen years.

> *And behold, there was a woman who had a spirit of infirmity eighteen years, and was bent over and could in no way raise herself up* (Luke 13:11).

Jesus saw the woman and took action. *"But when Jesus saw her, He called her to Him and said to her, 'Woman, you are loosed from your infirmity'"* (Luke 13:12). It is interesting that once again there was no interview, no pointing of fingers, no asking of questions, and no assumption that she was sick due to the dealings of God.

Jesus laid His hands on this suffering woman and she was instantly healed. He then said something interesting. *"So ought not this woman, being a daughter of Abraham, whom Satan has bound—think of it—for eighteen years, be loosed from this bond on the Sabbath?"* (Luke 13:16). Notice that her suffering was caused by Satan, and Jesus referred to her healing as being "loosed" from bondage.

Sickness is not abundant life. Sickness was not the purpose of God in Eden, and will not be found in heaven. Jesus healed all who came to Him regardless of the reason for their sickness. Jesus opposed sickness in His earthly ministry and His heart for those who suffer is no different now.

> *And He entered the synagogue again, and a man was there who had a withered hand. So they watched Him closely, whether He would heal him on the Sabbath, so that they might accuse Him. And He said to the man who had the withered hand, "Step forward." Then He said to them, "Is it lawful on the Sabbath to do good or to do evil, to save life or to kill?" But they kept silent. And when He had looked around at them with anger, being grieved by the hardness of their hearts, He said to the man, "Stretch out your hand." And he stretched it out, and his hand was restored as whole as the other* (Mark 3:1-5).

In this amazing story we find Jesus confronted with another healing opportunity on the Sabbath day. Jesus' words are often misunderstood, so let's pay close attention. *"Is it lawful on the Sabbath to do good or to do evil, to save life or to kill?"* Do you see it? Jesus is in danger of being accused of breaking the Sabbath to heal, but he responds and compares refusing to heal the man to doing evil and killing! In other words, not healing the man, regardless of the day, would be evil and likened to killing! This gives us an amazing look at the heart of God with respect to healing. If refusing to heal is evil, then healing is obviously good.

> *How God anointed Jesus of Nazareth with the Holy Spirit and with power, who went about doing good and healing all who were oppressed by the devil, for God was with Him* (Acts 10:38).

In this well-known Scripture, doing good and healing are linked. Sickness is identified as the oppression of the devil.

> *...For this purpose the Son of God was manifested, that He might destroy the works of the devil* (1 John 3:8).

When we look at the ministry of Jesus, we see Him healing multitudes of sick people. Sickness was a work of the enemy that Jesus came to destroy! Sickness is not a tool that God needs to accomplish His purpose. In fact, His purpose is to destroy sickness! Until we comprehend God's heart for His people and understand His view of sickness, we will struggle to believe and receive.

The words found in the Bible that reveal God's opinion of sickness include: bondage, cursed, captive, brokenhearted, infirm, bound by Satan, afflicted by evil, and oppressed of the devil. *There are no verses that describe sickness as a blessing from God.* Sickness is not in His nature. Healing is His nature. He wants you to be well!

Every good gift and every perfect gift is from above, *and comes down from the Father of lights, with whom there is no variation or shadow of turning* (James 1:17).

It is sad that so many believers have misunderstood the heart of God and attribute to Him what is actually the work and nature of the enemy! No wonder so many Christians are suffering. Just as Jesus came to do the Father's will, and the Father only gives good gifts, Jesus went about doing good and healing all. He has made healing available to all. It is your redemptive right to be healed!

GOD'S LOVING WILL

Healing is an expression of love. Any parent will recognize their own human love and compassion for a child who is sick. No parent in their right mind will agree that a suffering child is a good thing and something to be embraced as God's loving will.

If sickness is God's will, or if sickness could be "allowed" by God for some divine purpose, then why do we seek medical help? There is an inconsistency in thinking that sickness may be God's will or mysterious purpose for my life, but I will seek medical assistance to see if I can alleviate the suffering. If you believe God wants you sick, then shouldn't you let sickness take its course and teach you what it needs to teach you? Nonsense makes sense to many religious minds!

When the same Christian parents who believe that sickness is a tool of God are faced with their child being sick, they don't declare that the sickness is from God. The parents will immediately do anything in their power to bring healing to their child. They will spare no expense for a suffering little one. Why would some then confidently pronounce that the sickness of an adult might be God's will? Aren't we God's children? What is the age at which the sick can no longer count on God's heart for healing and must now change their theology to accept sickness as from God?

To be sure, many agree that sickness at face value is not a good thing, and that doctors have been given by God to help us recover. There is nothing wrong with doctors and hospitals, but what if their help is insufficient? Do we then become theological about the circumstance and conclude that because science is limited, this sickness must be from God? The science of a hundred years ago was vastly less effective than today and many died in the past who would have lived today. Did God have a role in these deaths?

If doctors and medicine are His answer, why have they been historically ineffective and even today unable to cure many diseases? At what point do we decide that a sickness is from God? Must we exhaust all medical possibilities before we put ourselves in His hands? The inconsistencies in this line of thinking are huge.

HEALING PRAYER

Father, I agree with Your Word that sickness is not Your will for my life—it is not a blessing and it is not my teacher! Amen!

Chapter 4

Healing in Redemption

In the beginning of this book I told the story of my revelation of healing in 1989 while in Guatemala. I had a revelation of Isaiah 53:5:

> *But He was wounded for our transgressions, He was bruised for our iniquities; the chastisement for our peace was upon Him, and by His stripes we are healed.*

That revelation was a seed that has continued to produce fruit in my life. Spiritual revelation often has layers of understanding that we progressively see as we journey through life. That has certainly been the case with me, and no doubt I have more to learn. I want to share with you the power of redemption and what the cross means for your life and health.

THE ROOT OF SIN

In order to understand God's will in healing, we must understand where sickness came from and what its root is.

Therefore, just as through one man sin entered the world, and death through sin... (Romans 5:12).

Sin and death are linked. Sin entered the world through man and death was the result. When we speak of death, we are speaking of the full spectrum of loss, corruption, tragedy, heartache, depression, anxiety, fear, and every other condition that afflicts humanity. Sickness is a consequence of the death unleashed by Adam and Eve. Sickness exists to hasten death.

Every sickness has as its goal the death of the sick one. If a common cold could kill you, it would. In fact, for those who are weak for other reasons, a cold can be fatal. There is no sickness that strengthens, blesses, or enhances the life of the sick one. Sickness will lead to premature death if given the opportunity.

Sin in the human race is the root of sickness. Apart from sin, sickness and death would not exist. Please understand that I am not referring to personal sin at this point. Adam's sin unleashed death, and sickness is a product of the power of death in humanity. God's original intent was that man eat from the Tree of Life and live forever (Genesis 2:9 and 3:22).

However, Adam's choice of independence from God—eating of the tree of the knowledge of good and evil—unleashed death and all its consequences. Mortality began, and a mortal body in a fallen world became subject to the impact of sin and corruption. Nothing has been the same since.

If we can understand sickness as a fruit of sin, then we can understand that sin is the root that must be dealt with. If the root of sin can be destroyed, the fruit of sickness has no source of spiritual authority in our bodies.

Let's look at the unholy union of sin and sickness in the Bible.

> *Bless the Lord, O my soul, and forget not all His benefits: who forgives all your iniquities, who heals all your diseases* (Psalm 103:2-3).

David understood the connection between sin and sickness and could foresee humanity's future deliverance from both the root and the fruit. When iniquities are forgiven, diseases can be healed.

> *Surely He has borne our griefs and carried our sorrows; yet we esteemed Him stricken, smitten by God, and afflicted. But He was wounded for our transgressions, He was bruised for our iniquities; the chastisement for our peace was upon Him, and by His stripes we are healed* (Isaiah 53:4-5).

While there is much debate over this passage by those who question healing as part of redemption, there is no debate that He was bruised for our iniquities and by His stripes we are healed, whatever that may mean. The question may arise as to whether this is talking about physical sicknesses or "spiritual sicknesses." Some will attempt to understand the significance of the cross as only spiritual. Is there any evidence that God was providing for physical needs as well?

Matthew quotes Isaiah during the ministry of Jesus.

> *When evening had come, they brought to Him many who were demon-possessed. And He cast out the spirits with a word, and healed all who were sick, that it might be fulfilled which was spoken by Isaiah the prophet, saying: "He Himself took our infirmities and bore our sicknesses"* (Matthew 8:16-17).

This is most definitely referring to physical sicknesses. The passage in Isaiah is referring to the ministry of Jesus healing those suffering physically. Jesus forgave sin and healed the sick in His earthly ministry as a demonstration of His will, His love, and the Kingdom that He announced through the gospel. If we can still receive forgiveness today, then healing is also available. They are inseparable in the salvation message.

After Jesus arose from the dead and sat down at the right hand of God, *all* who went to the church in Jerusalem in Acts chapter 5 were healed. How do we explain this if physical healing is no longer available? The Great Commission to go into all the world, preach the gospel, and lay hands on the sick so that they recover are all promises for the church age. The gifts of healing given to the church in 1 Corinthians 12:9 are for the church age as discussed earlier.

> *So that you come short in no gift, eagerly waiting for the revelation of our Lord Jesus Christ* (1 Corinthians 1:7).

The stripes upon Jesus were for our physical healing. Some insist that physical healing may be inferred in Isaiah 53, but that part of the prophecy was fulfilled in the ministry of Jesus and is no longer valid. The problem with this line of reasoning is that Jesus also forgave sin in His earthly ministry.

Is the forgiveness of sin no longer valid as well? We need to be consistent. The truth is that Jesus was demonstrating the Kingdom, which was ushered in on the day of Pentecost and which provides both forgiveness and healing for all who believe. He forgives all our iniquities and heals all our diseases.

Let us take a closer look at Isaiah 53:4-5. The following is a more literal rendering of these verses from the Hebrew language:

- "Surely, He has borne our diseases and carried our pains"

- "But He was pierced for our transgressions"

- "He was crushed for our iniquities"

- "With His wounds we are healed." (Rapha)

As mentioned earlier, the word *Rapha* is one of the redemptive names of God revealed in the Old Testament. *"I am the Lord who heals* [Jehovah Rapha] *you"* (Exodus 15:26). *"By His stripes we are healed"* (Isaiah 53:5). His name is Rapha, the Lord our Healer. Just as He is our righteousness and bore our sins, He is our Healer and bore our sicknesses. Just as God is eternal, His redemptive names reveal His eternal nature. For healing to disappear, God would have to cease being God.

Isaiah 53:10 declares, *"Yet it pleased the Lord to bruise Him; He has put Him to grief."* In the Hebrew it becomes even more clear: "Yet it pleased the Lord to crush Him; He hath made Him weak, sick, diseased."

This is what Jesus suffered on the cross for us! Were these "spiritual diseases"? No. Jesus took upon Himself all the sicknesses of mankind at the same moment that He was being made sin for us.

> *For He made Him who knew no sin to be sin for us, that we might become the righteousness of God in Him* (2 Corinthians 5:21).

The root of sin and the fruit of sickness were both carried to the cross so that we could be free from both. It would be confusing to have sin carried to the cross to redeem mankind from its power and eternal death, but simultaneously leave humans at the mercy of sickness, which was a result of Adam's sin.

HUMAN MORTALITY

I understand that we are mortal and unless Jesus returns first, we will all die. Mortality is obviously a result of Adam's sin, but must we die sick? Is death only a result of sickness, or is it a result of the aging process of mortality?

> *For as the body without the spirit is dead...* (James 2:26).

Death occurs when the spirit leaves the body. Sickness only hastens the corruption of mortality. It is not necessary to die sick. Our bodies will wear out due to mortality, but they need not die from disease.

Isaiah 53:11 declares, *"for he shall bear their iniquities."* The word for "bear" is the Hebrew word *nasa*. Earlier, in Isaiah 53:4, He bore our *"griefs,"* our diseases. The Hebrew word for bore/bear is *nasa*. Whatever Jesus did with sin, He did with sickness. He bore them both. When the power of sin was defeated on the cross, the power of sickness lost its authority.

> *For the law of the **Spirit of life in Christ Jesus** has made me **free from the law of sin and death*** (Romans 8:2).

I hope you will stop and meditate on this verse. This is one of the most powerful verses in the Bible and describes in a very few words the incredible work of redemption. The law of sin and death is not referring to the Law of Moses. It is referring to God's original commandment to Adam and Eve.

> *And the Lord God commanded the man, saying, "Of every tree of the garden you may freely eat; but of the tree of the knowledge of good and evil you shall not eat, for in the day that you eat of it you shall surely die"* (Genesis 2:16-17).

Adam unleashed death, and with it every calamity that transpires on the earth. The *"law of sin and death"* could be described as independence from God that results in darkness, loss, corruption, poverty, sickness, tragedy, and death.

What is *"the law of the Spirit of life in Christ Jesus?"* It is the new creation that is now available by faith in the redemptive work of Jesus on the cross.

> *Therefore, if **anyone is in Christ**, he is a **new creation**; old things have passed away; behold, all things have become new* (2 Corinthians 5:17).

In other words, those who choose to believe in and receive the life of Christ become new creations who are no longer subject to the law of sin and death! This does not mean that mortality doesn't exist. The redemption of our mortal bodies is a future event, but the law of death that allows sickness and disease has been broken! We can be as free from sin and sickness as we choose to be.

> *But if the Spirit of Him who raised Jesus from the dead dwells in you, He who raised Christ from the dead will also give life to your mortal bodies through His Spirit who dwells in you* (Romans 8:11).

There it is! If the Spirit who raised Jesus from the dead lives in you, though we are mortal, His Spirit will give life to us! If you can grasp this truth, you will see that you are just as healed as you are forgiven. It only takes one "revelation" from God to set you free from whatever afflicts you. Please take time to meditate and pray over these verses. There is grace for you.

> *Who Himself bore our sins in His own body on the tree, that we, having died to sins, might live for righteousness—by whose stripes you were healed* (1 Peter 2:24).

Peter quotes Isaiah and the union of sin and sickness is confirmed again. Righteousness by faith has replaced the sin nature with the "new creation" man, and physical healing is a redemptive right. Again, some may question if this is referring to physical healing or "spiritual healing."

HEALING—A REDEMPTIVE RIGHT

When we look at the Greek word for "healed," which is *iaomai,* in 1 Peter 2:24, we find that it means "to cure, heal, and make whole." This word appears twenty-eight times in the New Testament and it refers specifically to physical healing at least twenty-three times. The other five instances imply physical healing. Physical healing was provided for by the stripes of Jesus.

Most would agree that God can heal if He wants to. But if divine healing exists at all, there must be a spiritual law that sustains it. God is not a God of whims. The mystery and confusion exist because not all experience healing in their bodies. The lack of visible evidence persuades them to believe that God chooses to heal some and not others. Thus begins the theological quagmire that steals the faith of so many and leaves them in suffering. When we base our faith on what we see, we limit the spiritual possibilities that God has given us.

When we look at the lives of some Christians or even our own lives, we may notice that though righteousness is a gift, not all act righteous. Paul even refers to carnal Christians in 1 Corinthians 3:1. Is God refusing to let them walk in righteousness for some mysterious reason? Just because some Christians still sin is not an argument against the gift of righteousness, and just because some are still sick is not an argument against the gift of healing. The issue isn't with God.

Let's continue to look at the relationship between sin and sickness for more understanding.

> *For I received from the Lord that which I also delivered to you: that the Lord Jesus on the same night in which He was betrayed took bread; and when He had given thanks, He broke it and said, "Take, eat; this is My body which is broken for you; do this in remembrance of Me." In the same manner He also took the cup after supper, saying, "This cup is the new covenant in My blood. This do, as often as you drink it, in remembrance of Me." For as often as you eat this bread and drink this cup, you proclaim the Lord's death till He comes* (1 Corinthians 11:23-26).

For most of the church, the blood of Jesus holds great significance. It is the blood that cleanses us from sin. We have redemption through His blood (Ephesians 1:7). We understand the significance of drinking the cup. By faith we are acknowledging the power of the blood that delivered us from the power of sin.

What about the bread? What does the eating of the bread signify? The bread was broken to represent His body. *"Take, eat; this is My body."* Does this have meaning for us? What role did His body play in our salvation? Let us go back to the first Passover when God was about to release the children of Israel from the bondage of Egypt.

Your lamb shall be without blemish, a male of the first year. ...Then the whole assembly of the congregation of Israel shall kill it at twilight. And they shall take some of the blood and put it on the two doorposts and on the lintel of the houses where they eat it. Then they shall eat the flesh on that night; roasted in fire, with unleavened bread and with bitter herbs they shall eat it. ...And thus you shall eat it: with a belt on your waist, your sandals on your feet, and your staff in your hand. So you shall eat it in haste. It is the Lord's Passover. ...Now the blood shall be a sign for you on the houses where you are. And when I see the blood, I will pass over you; and the plague shall not be on you to destroy you when I strike the land of Egypt (Exodus 12:5-13).

Without taking the time to develop the powerful significance of this event in detail, let us concentrate on two important aspects. The sacrificial lamb was a type of Christ that was to be slain, and its blood smeared on the doorposts of the house. This we clearly understand in light of the Lamb of God and His blood, which was shed for our deliverance from sin—a type and shadow of bondage and slavery in Egypt.

But why did they eat the lamb? The body of the lamb was consumed by the people even though the blood was the sign of deliverance from the curse of death. Let us go to Psalms for the answer. The psalmist reflected upon Israel's deliverance from Egypt and recounted the events of that time.

He also destroyed all the firstborn in their land, the first of all their strength. He also brought them

*out with silver and gold, and there was none feeble
among His tribes* (Psalm 105:36-37).

He brought Israel forth from the slavery of Egypt with silver and gold, and there was not one feeble person among several million people! The word "feeble" means to falter or waver, to be decayed, to fail or to be weak. The masses of people who left Egypt by the power of God were not feeble! They were not sick! Why not? Because they had eaten the lamb. They had partaken of the body that was broken for them.

Can this Old Testament type and shadow be more powerful for Israel than the reality of Christ's body is for the church? I believe not: *"Take, eat; this is My body, which is broken for you." "By His stripes we were healed." "Who forgives all your iniquities and heals all your diseases."*

Jesus dealt with the root—sin—with His blood. He dealt with the fruit—sickness—with His body. The shed blood destroyed the power of sin and brought forgiveness to mankind. His body that bore stripes for our healing deals with the manifestation of sickness and suffering that sin unleashed.

Redemption is a legal issue. God does not choose to forgive some and not others. God chose to redeem all of mankind from the curse of sin and offer forgiveness to whosoever will receive it. In the same way, healing for physical suffering is also offered. If the root of sin has been defeated, the fruit of sickness has no spiritual authority.

If Jesus bore our sins and He bore our sicknesses, then neither sin nor sickness should have dominion over us. If we can resist the devil and he will flee, we can resist his evil works as well!

HEALING PRAYER

Father, quicken me to see the breadth and depth of Your redemptive work through Jesus on the cross. May I truly see my sins and all sickness taken by Him on my behalf. I choose to believe and receive Your full redemptive power now, in the name of Jesus. Amen!

Chapter 5

Redeemed from the Curse

We have already seen how the Bible refers to sickness as a curse. Sadly, many Christians still believe that the curse might be a blessing in disguise. Until we have God's attitude toward sickness, and we understand the price that Jesus paid to free us from sin and sickness, we will continue to be double-minded and unable to receive from God.

In the book of Numbers, we find an amazing story of rebellion, grace, and healing as Israel wandered in the wilderness. It is a perfect picture of redemption and is directly related to Jesus and the cross.

> *And the people spoke against God and against Moses: "Why have you brought us up out of Egypt to die in the wilderness? For there is no food and no water, and our soul loathes this worthless bread." So the Lord sent fiery serpents among the people, and they bit the people; and many of the people of Israel died. Therefore the people came to Moses, and said, "We have sinned, for we have spoken*

against the Lord and against you; pray to the Lord that He take away the serpents from us." So Moses prayed for the people. Then the Lord said to Moses, "Make a fiery serpent, and set it on a pole; and it shall be that everyone who is bitten, when he looks at it, shall live." So Moses made a bronze serpent, and put it on a pole; and so it was, if a serpent had bitten anyone, when he looked at the bronze serpent, he lived (Numbers 21:5-9).

The people of Israel were complaining against Moses and against God's provision for them in the wilderness. God sent serpents into their midst and many were bitten and died. The people then repented, and Moses prayed to God. Under the Old Covenant, rebellious behavior had dire consequences. Don't let that confuse you. Under the New Covenant we are not under the Law of blessings and curses, but we can learn from these examples.

It is interesting that the Lord commanded Moses to make a serpent of brass to put on a pole, and all who gazed upon the brass serpent would live. What is the significance of this event? Why would God insist on lifting up that which was the problem, the serpent, on a pole in order to bring healing to His people? Jesus gave us the answer:

And as Moses lifted up the serpent in the wilderness, even so must the Son of Man be lifted up, that whoever believes in Him should not perish but have eternal life (John 3:14-15).

Many years later after the event with Israel in the desert, Jesus compared Himself to the serpent on the pole! Why?

Wouldn't it be better to identify Himself as the sacrificial Lamb? Jesus certainly was and is the Lamb of God, but when He was lifted up on the cross something incredible took place. Just as the brass serpent was a representation of the curse of serpents among the people of Israel, Jesus became identified with the curse of sin in the human race.

> *Christ has redeemed us from the curse of the law, having become a curse for us (for it is written, "Cursed is everyone who hangs on a tree")* (Galatians 3:13).

As explained in the Law of blessings and curses found in Deuteronomy 28, the curse of the law included every sickness and distress known to man.

> *If you do not carefully observe all the words of this law that are written in this book, that you may fear this glorious and awesome name, THE LORD YOUR GOD, then the Lord will bring upon you and your descendants extraordinary plagues—great and prolonged plagues—and serious and prolonged sicknesses. Moreover He will bring back on you all the diseases of Egypt, of which you were afraid, and they shall cling to you. Also every sickness and every plague, which is not written in this Book of the Law, will the Lord bring upon you until you are destroyed* (Deuteronomy 28:58-61).

Again, these curses were a result of rebelling against the Lord under the Law of Moses. It is a specific context that reveals what is meant by the curse. Galatians 3:13 declares that Christ was made a curse on the cross! He became that which afflicted humanity. Why? That whosoever believes in Him should not perish. All who believe in the One hanging on the cross shall live.

> *For He made Him who knew no sin to be sin for us, that we might become the righteousness of God in Him* (2 Corinthians 5:21).

Until we fully grasp what this means, redemption and healing will remain mysteries. Jesus became a curse and became sin for us on the cross that we might be fully, legally redeemed from the power of sin and all of its manifestations, including sickness. The event with the serpents in the wilderness was given as an example in order that New Covenant believers would understand the power of the cross! Many years later, Paul wrote in the New Testament the following:

> *Now these things became our examples, to the intent that we should not lust after evil things as they also lusted. …nor let us tempt Christ, as some of them also tempted, and were destroyed by serpents; nor complain, as some of them also complained, and were destroyed by the destroyer. Now all these things happened to them as examples, and they were written for our admonition, upon whom the ends of the ages have come* (1 Corinthians 10:6-11).

When Jesus referred to Himself as a type of the serpent being lifted up, He was revealing a powerful truth. That which was unleashed by Adam and has afflicted mankind ever since was fully, totally, and completely dealt with on the cross. When the power of sin was destroyed, its many manifestations lost their authority. We have been freed to live the life God intended. The story of the serpent on the cross was written for our admonition!

We have been taught about the sin issue. Most Christians understand the topic of the blood and the atoning sacrifice for sin. But many have never grasped that if the root of sin has been dealt with, all that sin has unleashed in mankind has lost its authority! If we can be made righteous and clean before God, then that righteousness is much more powerful than sin and sickness! Sickness has lost its authority. Sickness is as defeated as sin is.

> *For the law of the Spirit of life in Christ Jesus has made me free from the law of sin and death* (Romans 8:2).

If you have partaken of His life by the Spirit, whether you know it or not you are free from the power of sin and free from the power of sickness! This is a legal act that delivered humanity from the impact of Adam's sin.

However, it remains for us to believe and receive it. Freedom from the power of sin does not mean that all choose to live free from sin. Freedom from the power of sickness is also a choice that many have not grasped or chosen to walk in. That which has been accomplished for mankind on the cross must be understood and appropriated by faith.

SALVATION AND HEALING

We must take the subject of healing out of the realm of "If it be Thy will," and submit ourselves to the fact that salvation and healing are the will of God and are available to all who believe.

Let's look at the word "salvation."

> *For God did not send His Son into the world to condemn the world, but that the world through Him might be saved* (John 3:17).

Saved is the Greek word *sozo* meaning "to save, keep safe and sound, to rescue from danger or destruction. To save a suffering one (from perishing), i.e., one suffering from disease, to make well, heal, restore to health. To preserve one who is in danger of destruction, to save or rescue."

Jesus became a curse and became sin on the cross for us that we might be delivered from destruction, rescued, made well, restored to health, and preserved! Can you see that salvation includes more than the forgiveness of sins and eternal life?

How is the word "saved" used in the New Testament? The following are some examples:

> *And she will bring forth a Son, and you shall call His name JESUS, for He will save His people from their sins* (Matthew 1:21).

Here the word "save," *sozo*, is used to describe salvation from sin.

*Then His disciples came to Him and awoke Him,
saying, "Lord, save us! We are perishing!"* (Matthew 8:25)

In this case we find *sozo* meaning to deliver from danger.

*And He said to her, "Daughter, your faith has made
you well. Go in peace, and be healed of your affliction"* (Mark 5:34).

In Mark 5, *sozo* is translated as "healed" referring to a
physical healing. The woman with the issue of blood was
physically healed.

Returning to John 3:17, it says, *"God sent not His Son into
the world to condemn the world, but that the world through
Him might be saved"*—sozo, meaning delivered, preserved,
and healed!

Salvation includes all aspects of our dilemma—spirit, soul,
and body. Healing is a legal part of redemption and available
to all who believe. If healing is not part of redemption, a different Greek word would have been chosen and the evidence
for physical healing in the New Testament would have been
explained as a temporary phenomenon.

If the type and shadow of Christ on the cross, the serpent on the pole, was sufficient to heal the children of
Israel physically, shouldn't we believe that Jesus Himself,
who accomplished redemption for us and became sin and
a curse for us, has provided both spiritual and physical salvation for the world? Is the Old Covenant better than the
New? I think not.

But now He has obtained a more excellent ministry, inasmuch as He is also Mediator of a better covenant, which was established on better promises (Hebrews 8:6).

Our new covenant in Jesus Christ is far more effective and powerful than the old covenant of the Law. As born-again, guilt-free children of God, we have access to all of the promises that redemption offers. Healing is our right.

HEALING PRAYER

Father, I thank You that You have freed me from the curse of sin and sickness. I receive Your finished work in my body and declare that healing is mine! Amen!

Chapter 6

Why Are We Sick?

I have spoken with many sincere believers who know that healing is a New Covenant right and they believe, confess, declare, and do whatever they think might work in order to be healed. I have done this. I have wondered at times why I was sick, or why I was not healed. I think we have established that the legal side of redemption includes healing, but what we know in our minds sometimes does not translate to our experience. How can we bridge the gap?

In Jesus' day, sickness seems to have been very common. Great crowds followed Him to be healed: *"...And great multitudes followed Him, and He healed them all"* (Matthew 12:15).

In Israel, in spite of the promises of blessing established in the Law of Moses and the steps to receive healing, multitudes were sick. While Jesus didn't spend time investigating why so many were sick, He did give us some insight within the context of Israel's relationship with God.

> *For the hearts of this people have grown dull. Their ears are hard of hearing, and their eyes they have closed, lest they should see with their eyes and hear*

> *with their ears, lest they should understand with*
> *their hearts and turn, so that I should heal them*
> (Matthew 13:15).

The problem was hardness of heart. Though the covenant of the Law provided healing for all in Israel, and though the Passover lamb was a type of Christ that brought healing to Israel many years before, it was the heart of the people that was the true problem. Hardness of heart, unwillingness to hear, and closed eyes are all reasons that multitudes in Israel were sick.

As we have seen earlier, sin entered the human race through Adam, and mortality was the result. Sickness and death are the fruit of Adam's sin. I am not referring to individual sin right now, but rather to the impact of sin in humans. There were no genetic defects, no horrible cancers, there was no heart disease, no Alzheimer's, no blindness or deafness, and no death until sin entered the world. Sin came first. Sicknesses came second.

> *Now may the God of peace Himself sanctify you*
> *completely; and may your whole spirit, soul, and*
> *body be preserved blameless at the coming of our*
> *Lord Jesus Christ* (1 Thessalonians 5:23).

Humans consist of spirit, soul, and body. The impact of sin is not limited to the physical body. People can suffer on other levels as well. The immediate impact of Adam's sin was to unplug mankind from God in the spiritual sense. The human spirit became independent from the Source of life—it was fallen and could not fight against the power and corruption of sin on any level. The independent spirit became subject to the desires of the flesh, the body, and soul. Mankind could still respond to God and the Old Testament is full of such stories; but apart from hearing a direct word from God, the human spirit was subject to the soul and flesh.

The soul, usually understood as the mind, will, emotions, and personality, became subject to distress. Mental anguish and depression are common symptoms in many today, which can be understood as sickness on the level of the soul. Emotional breakdowns are also common due to sin in the world. Outbursts of anger, bitterness, strife, lust, greed, pride, and other such emotions can do great damage.

WHOLE HEALING

Healing isn't just about the physical body! Humans are beings consisting of spirit, soul, and body—and all of those areas can suffer. And, all those areas can be healed and enjoy health. Being born again not only heals our spirits, it is a "new creation" created in righteousness who is one with Him (2 Corinthians 5:17, 1 Corinthians 6:17).

But we are not only spirit. We also have a soul and a body. Mental anguish can give birth to emotional breakdowns and physical sicknesses. Physical sickness can create mental and emotional symptoms. When one area of our being suffers, the other areas become candidates for suffering as well. Many times a healing from emotional trauma can bring physical healing. We will consider the subject of trauma in a later chapter.

The glaring fact is, even born-again Christians can continue to suffer. Being born again does not make all suffering disappear. Jesus declared that in this world we would have tribulation:

> ...*In the world you will have tribulation; but be of good cheer, I have overcome the world* (John 16:33).

Jesus was speaking of persecution for our faith and the challenge of living in a fallen world. While persecution was promised, sickness was not. Sickness is not the kind of suffering that Jesus or the New Testament writers referred to when they spoke of suffering. Thank God that Jesus has overcome the consequences of sin and that by faith we can enter into His victory!

That which has been made available through the cross must be accessed by faith. Though you are a new creation, created in righteousness, free from the power of sin, you can still choose to sin. Though you are a born-again Christian who believes that by His stripes you were healed, you can still be sick. The benefits of redemption are not always automatic. Like seeking a financial inheritance that may be tied up in the courts, there are often steps that must be taken in order to receive what is legally ours. In our case, it is simply an issue of understanding and believing.

WISDOM AND GRACE

Understanding why we may be sick could help in bringing the healing that we need. I am very aware that Jesus didn't question those He healed in order to pinpoint the source of their suffering. However, His statement about the hardened heart is revealing (Matthew 13:15). It won't hurt for us to consider some of the possibilities for sickness that we may have ignored or grown hardened toward. Wisdom from God can be part of the healing we seek.

Please remember that there is grace for every need and every sickness. The source of sickness won't stop the grace of God, but it is possible that the source of the sickness may hinder the expectation of health and peace. Ultimately, the source of sickness is Adam's sin. That revelation alone can heal you. But perhaps there are some issues in our lives that are the result of Adam's sin and can be addressed in order to receive the healing that is ours.

The two subjects that often stir the most negative reaction in the subject of healing are when we speak of personal sin and personal faith. These two subjects are "sacred cows" to many, so I am very aware that there may be some resistance to the following discussion. Nevertheless, if we aren't willing to be brutally honest with ourselves, we will only delay the healing that is so readily available.

POSSIBLE OPEN DOORS FOR SICKNESS

Personal Sin

According to Jesus, it is possible for personal sin to be the cause of a physical affliction. Personal sin is simply a symptom of Adam's original sin. In the story of the man at the pool of Bethesda, we find Jesus ministering to an individual who had been suffering for thirty-eight years (John 5:1-4). After being healed, the man later encountered Jesus in the temple. Jesus said to him, *"See, you have been made well. Sin no more, lest a worse thing come upon you"* (John 5:14). The implication is clear. Personal sin holds the potential for sickness and even worse things. The fact that Jesus said, *"Sin no more,"* implies that it was this man's sin that was the problem in the first place. Sin didn't stop the healing, but it was the cause of the sickness. There was grace for this man, followed by an admonition.

Can you get venereal disease if you and your spouse have never engaged in sex with others before or after marriage? No. Can you get lung cancer from smoking if you never smoke? No. We could go on listing a number of physical issues that are directly related to our personal choices. The consequences of our choices are due to Adam's sin; but nonetheless, our choices allowed the consequences to enter our lives.

It is possible that our personal lifestyles are open doors to sickness and disease. Paul speaks of sowing to the flesh and says the following, *"For he who sows to his flesh will of the flesh reap corruption…"* (Galatians 6:8).

This principle can be applied to all aspects of our lives. Sowing to the flesh can speak of our morals, our integrity, our lifestyles, indulging our feelings, poor diet, etc. Corruption can come in many forms, and sickness would certainly be a possibility.

Let me be clear that not all sicknesses are the result of personal sin. Sin in the human race is the root of all sickness, but not all sickness can be traced to personal sin. However, as Jesus pointed out to the man at Bethesda, personal sin can be the source of the problem.

Let's consider some other possibilities in our lives that could be an open door for sickness. What does it mean to sow to the flesh? Strife in our relationships certainly falls in this category.

Strife and Division

But if you have bitter envy and self-seeking in your hearts, do not boast and lie against the truth. This wisdom does not descend from above, but is earthly, sensual, demonic. For where envy and self-seeking exist, confusion and every evil thing are there (James 3:14-16).

Strife in our relationships will not only create mental and emotional stress but can also lead to physical problems. In this same epistle of James, we find his conclusion for those who are sick:

Confess your trespasses to one another, and pray for one another, that you may be healed... (James 5:16).

When we read the book of James in context, you can find a number of exhortations about the strife and fighting among them (see James 4). I don't think it would be wrong to say that some of the sickness in their midst was a result of strife. For that reason, James exhorts the confessing of faults one to another. When we cease to be an accuser and decide to be an intercessor for those with whom we have contention, we create an environment for healing. Jesus taught about this as well:

> *But I say to you, love your enemies, bless those who curse you, do good to those who hate you, and pray for those who spitefully use you and persecute you* (Matthew 5:44).

Strife is certainly a symptom of the flesh out of control. *"Every evil thing"* can have strife and bitterness as its source. Sickness can certainly be considered an evil thing.

I have known many who have lived lives of strife and bitterness who later struggled with chronic ailments. While my observations are not scientific, I have no doubt there can be a correlation. I am not saying that this will hold true for every person every time, but it is a possibility.

This same theme can be found in 1 Corinthians:

> *For first of all, when you come together as a church, I hear that there are divisions among you...* (1 Corinthians 11:18).

Paul's letter of 1 Corinthians contains a number of corrections and exhortations for this group. In chapter 11 he addresses the strife in their midst. Let's follow the story in this chapter.

> *For in eating, each one takes his own supper ahead of others; and one is hungry and another is drunk. What! Do you not have houses to eat and*

drink in? Or do you despise the church of God and shame those who have nothing? What shall I say to you? Shall I praise you in this? I do not praise you (1 Corinthians 11:21-22).

The custom in the early church was for the believers to gather around a meal that included what we now know as "communion." In the Corinthian church, a meal was the practice and there was much eating and drinking going on. From Paul's description we can find undisciplined behavior to the point of gluttony and drunkenness. The phrase, *"do you despise the church of God, and shame those who have nothing,"* is at the heart of his exhortation. The self-centeredness and attitude of some toward others in the church was an open door for what James described as *"confusion and every evil thing."* What are the results of such behavior?

> *For he who eats and drinks in an unworthy manner eats and drinks judgment to himself, not discerning the Lord's body.* **For this reason** *many are weak and sick among you, and many sleep* (1 Corinthians 11:29-30).

Eating and drinking in an unworthy manner is a direct reference to the selfish gluttony, drunkenness, and shaming of those who had nothing. Such carnal behavior in this time of communion with the body of Christ was self-condemning to those who were guilty of this conduct. *"For this reason"* many were sick and even dead!

Not discerning the Lord's body can have another profound connotation. We have already discussed His body suffering the stripes, His beatings, for our healing. When we do not discern the finished work of the cross, an area of unbelief still has a place in our hearts. More on that later.

It is possible that sickness can gain access to our bodies through strife, selfishness, and any divisions that we may have allowed or created in our lives. If sin is the root of all sickness in the human race, then personal sin can certainly be a possible cause of our infirmities. It must be considered.

Praise God that His mercies are new every morning and we can come boldly before the throne of grace and restore our relationship with the Father and with others! (See Lamentations 3:22-23 and Hebrews 4:16.)

Self-Centeredness

It is interesting to consider Isaiah 58 in this discussion. We have seen how self-centeredness and strife can create an environment for sickness, but let's see the impact of a life lived to bless others.

> *Is this not the fast that I have chosen: to loose the bonds of wickedness, to undo the heavy burdens, to let the oppressed go free, and that you break every yoke? Is it not to share your bread with the hungry, and that you bring to your house the poor who are cast out; when you see the naked, that you cover him, and not hide yourself from your own flesh? Then your light shall break forth like the morning, your healing shall spring forth speedily...* (Isaiah 58:6-8).

This passage in Isaiah 58 is an interesting revelation of God's view of the fast that He has chosen. In verses 6-8 we find praise for a life that is concerned about others. One of the results of such a lifestyle of giving and serving is that *"your healing shall spring forth speedily."* In other words, self-centeredness is not an environment for health and healing. Those who simply live for themselves, seeking to satisfy their lusts and desires, are more likely to reap corruption than those who are giving themselves to bless others.

> *For he who sows to his flesh will of the flesh reap corruption, but he who sows to the Spirit will of the Spirit reap everlasting life* (Galatians 6:8).

This coincides very well with Jesus' statement on the power of giving. Those who give, receive.

> *Give, and it will be given to you: good measure, pressed down, shaken together, and running over will be put into your bosom...* (Luke 6:38).

As we give to others, our own needs get met, including the need for healing. Self-centeredness is an opportunity for sickness. It allows the "death" of Adam's sin an opportunity in our lives.

When we choose to live for others and allow the love of God to guide us to be a blessing, healing shall spring forth! No doubt this would include healing on every level—mental, emotional, and physical. The actions of love and sharing are the environment for health and healing. This is certainly alluded to in Peter's description of Jesus' ministry on earth.

God anointed Jesus of Nazareth with the Holy
Spirit and with power, who went about doing good
and healing all who were oppressed by the devil, for
God was with Him (Acts 10:38).

Doing good was the motivation for healing. Being a blessing will create an environment for health and healing because God is in that motivation.

We are looking at possible causes of sickness and have thus far considered personal sin, strife and self-centeredness. Let's move on to some other possibilities.

Diet

No longer drink only water, but use a little wine for
your stomach's sake and your frequent infirmities
(1 Timothy 5:23).

In this verse Paul is advising Timothy of what to do concerning his frequent stomach infirmities. This is an interesting verse because it reveals a number of things to us. Paul's first reaction was not to pray for Timothy or encourage Timothy to fast and pray. Paul understood Timothy's physical issues to have a natural reason that required a natural solution.

When I say "natural," I mean that the solution was not spiritual. We can assume that Timothy had been bothered by germs or parasites from bad drinking water. That is still common in many places in the world. The properties of wine could be a natural remedy for such contamination.

This situation brings us to the topic of the "natural" aspect of health and healing. Not all sicknesses stem from strife or personal sin. It could be that a poor diet is the culprit. Food is fuel for the body, and our bodies were designed to need certain nutrients and vitamins for optimum health. When the human body is denied proper nourishment or is fed with unhealthy foods, there can be health issues that arise.

We need to understand that sin in the world has impacted the food we eat. Food is not pristine and without the impact of corruption. How we approach our diets and our faith for food are important. Some disregard the issue of diet and claim they are eating "by faith." If so, they should be healthy.

Without getting into a full-blown discussion of diet, suffice it to say that many of the health issues in our country are due to poor food choices. Obesity, heart disease, and other physical maladies are many times the result of poor eating choices over years. Coupled with stress, strife, and other factors, diet can be an open door to health issues. Sowing and reaping impact our lives on this very basic level.

If you are not healthy and have frequent physical challenges, it could be the result of what you are eating. Prayer may not be the answer. Changing your diet might be the answer. Some tend to take better care of their cars than they do of their bodies!

Overeating is often a response to the body craving certain minerals, nutrients, and vitamins that it is not getting. When the body is not properly nourished, the response is often to keep eating. Food is fuel, and inadequate fuel will sooner or later create consequences.

Often what we want is a miracle healing, but what we need is a healthy lifestyle. *Choosing* health is frequently the key to the healing we seek.

A Spirit of Infirmity

And behold, there was a woman who had a spirit of infirmity eighteen years, and was bent over and could in no way raise herself up. But when Jesus saw her, He called her to Him and said to her, "Woman, you are loosed from your infirmity." And He laid His hands on her, and immediately she was made straight, and glorified God (Luke 13:11-13).

In this story, Jesus ministered to a woman who had been oppressed by a spirit of infirmity for eighteen years. The gospels speak several times of healings that involved a demonic presence in the life of the afflicted one.

When evening had come, they brought to Him many who were demon-possessed. And He cast out the spirits with a word, and healed all who were sick (Matthew 8:16).

God anointed Jesus of Nazareth with the Holy Spirit and with power, who went about doing good and healing all who were oppressed by the devil, for God was with Him (Acts 10:38).

Some sicknesses are demonic in nature. A spirit of infirmity is a demonic presence that afflicts a person mentally or physically. In the case of physical oppression, the body is impacted in a way that to the natural eye could seem to be a known, medical condition. If we took this woman to any doctor in the world, after x-rays and other tests no doubt her condition could have been described and diagnosed with medical terms. But there would be no remedy. No doctor would conclude that she had a spirit of infirmity. It is doubtful that any medically trained person on the earth would reach such a conclusion. Thus, the medical community in this case would be powerless to help. Medicine and surgery won't break the power of a spirit of infirmity.

Jesus saw something that no one else could see. Jesus saw a spiritual oppression that created a physical symptom. This woman had been oppressed by a spirit for eighteen years. X-rays would reveal a condition familiar to doctors. There would be medical terms and symptoms that could be seen. But when Jesus cast out the spirit of infirmity, all of the physical symptoms left with it! What seemed incurable left instantly!

Before assuming that an affliction is spiritual in nature, the other causes should be considered. Most of our sicknesses are self-induced. Of course, strife, bitterness, and personal sin could be possible opportunities for spirits of infirmity to enter into the picture. A spirit of infirmity can be cast out, but the impact of an unhealthy lifestyle can't. There is grace regardless of the immediate source of the sickness, but ongoing healthiness may require adjustments in our lifestyles.

Fear

And release those who through fear of death were all their lifetime subject to bondage (Hebrews 2:15).

One of the fundamental changes that took place in Adam and Eve after they sinned was that they were transformed from bearing the image of God—faith—to bearing the image of death and corruption—fear. After eating of the tree of the knowledge of good and evil, God appeared in the Garden in search of Adam and Eve.

Then the Lord God called to Adam and said to him, "Where are you?" So he said, "I heard Your voice in the garden, and I was afraid because I was naked; and I hid myself" (Genesis 3:9-10).

The voice of God, which should have given Adam and Eve great joy and peace, was now met with fear. They no longer bore the image of God. They were separated from His life. Death—separation—had taken place and mortality—death in the flesh—had begun. Sicknesses would soon manifest in humans.

The fear of death mentioned in Hebrews 2:15 is the birthplace of all fears. Fear is really faith in reverse. It is faith in the devil, faith in fallen humanity, and faith in fallen nature to do you harm. Fear comes by hearing the words of the world. It is stimulated through negative thoughts. It is expressed through words. Fear expects negative things. Fear is a force that attracts according to its nature—sin and death.

Many sicknesses are directly related to fear. Fear of disease is promoted continually on TV and in the media. The onslaught of new drugs with new side effects keeps many in a state of constant fear. Such anxiety opens the body up for sickness. You will attract what you expect. Faith and fear work in the same way but with opposite results. We will look at the subject of faith in more detail in a later chapter.

Fear of failure, fear of heights, fear of people, fear of the dark, fear of driving, etc. The list could go on and on. Every fear is a weakness in our soul that exposes us to the corruption of the world. Sickness is corruption.

> *There is no fear in love; but perfect love casts out fear, because fear involves torment. But he who fears has not been made perfect in love* (1 John 4:18).

Fear is an indication of not embracing the love of God in some area of our lives. The more we allow His love to overwhelm us, the less chance there is that fear will exist in our hearts. Healing is God's love in action, but fear can hinder the healing that is ours.

STRESS

> *Yet I considered it necessary to send to you Epaphroditus, my brother, fellow worker, and fellow soldier, but your messenger and the one who ministered to my need; since he was longing for you all, and was distressed because you had heard that*

*he was sick. **For indeed he was sick almost unto death; but God had mercy on him, and not only on him but on me also,** lest I should have sorrow upon sorrow. Therefore I sent him the more eagerly, that when you see him again you may rejoice, and I may be less sorrowful. Receive him therefore in the Lord with all gladness, and hold such men in esteem; because for the work of Christ he came close to death, not regarding his life, to supply what was lacking in your service toward me* (Philippians 2:25-30).

Epaphroditus, a friend and helper of Paul, was dedicated to taking care of Paul to such an extent that he overextended himself and became sick. In our way of thinking, he stressed out. He over-committed. He burned the candle at both ends. In our modern, multitasking society, many of us are challenged in this area. Stress, whether it deals with ministry or stems from the cares and concerns of job and family, is a powerful, negative force that can open the door to sickness.

When we allow stress to consume us, we are not regarding our lives. Burnout is common in our fast-paced lives, and burnout can put so much stress on the body that it begins to shut down or be unable to resist sickness. It may not be a prayer of faith that is needed, but a decision to take control of one's life and choose to establish limits on activities that create stress.

Not regarding our lives can also include choices that damage our bodies. Vices such as smoking, drinking, and illegal and even some legal drugs are toxic to our bodies and sow the seeds of corruption. The diseases that come from these activities steal life and potential. It doesn't mean that healing is not available, but it may be more difficult to be free of guilt and full of faith for those who have willingly chosen these activities.

If you feel that your lifestyle choices are probably the reason for your physical affliction, it can seem harder to receive from God. This doesn't mean it is hard for God. Healing is already available to all regardless of where the sickness came from. There is grace. It simply can complicate the sick person's faith. Feelings of unworthiness or guilt will always steal faith from our hearts.

In all of the areas I have mentioned, it must be understood that our healing and health have been provided for in *"the law of the Spirit of life in Christ Jesus"* (Romans 8:2). The more we understand the spiritual side of sin and sickness, the more we can cooperate with God's will for us. There is grace for every need.

HEALING PRAYER

Father, help me to see the root of any sickness or affliction in my life. Reveal to my heart Your wisdom for living in health on every level. I choose to guard my heart from strife, fear, self-centeredness, unhealthy desires, and stress. I receive Your grace of healing in Jesus' name! Amen!

Chapter 7

Physical and Emotional Trauma

Their son died at the age of 21 quite unexpectedly. It was a tragic accident that overwhelmed the parents with grief. Over time, the mother was able to transition into life without her son, but the father did not. He remained heart-broken and never came to a place of healing for his grief. He became moody, irritable, angry, and isolated. A couple of years went by and his health declined. He was diagnosed with cancer and lived less than a year from the time of the diagnosis.

I cannot prove the link between grief and sickness, but I know it is there. The trauma of losing a loved one can steal the will to live. Something has been lost that is irreplaceable; and rather than looking to the Lord for comfort and a renewed vision for life, some remained paralyzed in grief.

Trauma has become a serious symptom of life in a fallen world. Most of us have suffered from unexpected events that produced grief, sadness, fear, or acute anxiety. We can often move past these events with minimum long-term impact.

However, many people carry the wounds of trauma for years or even for the rest of their lives. Such emotional and mental wounds must be ministered to and healed. Jesus said:

> *The Spirit of the Lord is upon Me, because He has anointed Me to preach the gospel to the poor; He has sent Me to heal the brokenhearted, to proclaim liberty to the captives and recovery of sight to the blind, to set at liberty those who are oppressed; to proclaim the acceptable year of the Lord* (Luke 4:18-19).

Jesus is concerned about every aspect of your life—spirit, soul, and body. Jesus came to heal the brokenhearted. Healing isn't just about our bodies. Jesus cares for our hearts as well.

Trauma comes from a deeply distressing or disturbing experience. Trauma can include such things as the unexpected death of a loved one, a physical assault, witnessing a horrible crime, a divorce, surviving a natural disaster or accident, etc. The list can go on and on.

A physical injury can trigger emotional or mental distress. In a similar manner, a mental or emotional trauma can also trigger physical symptoms or even chronic sickness.

> *Beloved, I pray that you may prosper in all things and be in health, just as your soul prospers* (3 John 2).

Physical health can be directly impacted by emotional and mental distress. The soul of a person includes mental and emotional expression. We can think of our soul as how we relate to the world around us, and our spirit in terms of how we relate to God. While a believer may be in harmony with God in a spiritual sense—born again, a new creation—if the soul of the believer is not prospering, the door is open for physical problems to develop.

When we experience trauma that does not get ministered to and resolved, a chronic stress can develop in the mind and emotions. Acute trauma can range from the shock of a car accident to the diagnosis of a doctor or the loss of a prized possession. Chronic trauma can include long-term mental, physical, or emotional abuse. Any number of things can trigger mental or emotional stress.

It needs to be understood that we do live in a fallen, corrupt world due to sin in the earth, but humans were not created to live in such an environment. Peace with God, peace with others, and peace with creation was God's original design for mankind. Sadly, sin has dramatically changed the dynamics of the human experience. Loss and heartache are common experiences.

How we deal with mental, emotional, and physical challenges can play a significant role in our physical health and healing over time.

It is encouraging to know that Jesus came to heal the brokenhearted and bring deliverance to the captives. Those suffering the effects of chronic or acute trauma certainly fall into those categories. Healing is available. Healing from trauma is needed if the body is going to be able to resist or recover from trauma-induced sickness.

Those who are suffering from grief and trauma must understand that there are options. The love of God can minister to the hurting heart. There is still a purpose for life and something to give to bless others. Something has been lost, but there is still so much to give. The greatest weapon against loss is to give and let the Lord replenish you on every level.

> *Give, and it will be given to you: good measure, pressed down, shaken together, and running over will be put into your bosom...* (Luke 6:38).

This promise touches every area of life. What we give to God and give to others releases His grace to meet our needs whether they be emotional or physical.

Let the Word of God be your Source of life. You may pass from the corruption of this world into the joy of the Lord if you choose to. He came to bind up your broken heart, set you free, and heal your body.

> *Now the God of hope fill you with all joy and peace in believing, that you may abound in hope by the power of the Holy Spirit* (Romans 15:13).

God will fill you with all joy and peace through believing! Rather than being held captive by emotional and mental distress, start believing the Word of God and let it heal you from the inside out.

> *Come to Me, all you who labor and are heavy laden, and I will give you rest* (Matthew 11:28).

Being healed mentally and emotionally is often the key that unlocks physical healing. Health involves the whole person. It does little good to focus on physical healing if the root problem lies elsewhere. While there is grace for the healing power of God regardless of the source of the sickness, staying healed and healthy may require mental and emotional healing or lifestyle changes.

Healing from trauma may include forgiving others, or even choosing to understand that God was not at fault. Many wrongly harbor offenses against God not realizing that He did not cause or desire the event that provoked the anguish. God is *not* the thief who comes to steal, kill, and destroy.

> *For the Son of Man did not come to destroy men's lives but to save them...* (Luke 9:56).

Understanding the impact of trauma is important. Someone who is suffering physically for years could possibly be suffering emotionally as well. Healing the emotional wound might be the key to physical recovery.

HEALING PRAYER

Father, I come to You for healing in my heart. I know You are acquainted with my grief and I look to You for wholeness. I receive the ministry of the Holy Spirit in my life and I thank You for opening my heart and my eyes to see the future You have for me. I will walk in health in every part of my being. Amen!

Chapter 8

Weeds

We had a neighbor whose backyard adjoined ours, separated by a fence. During one summer season they apparently decided to no longer care for or water their yard. It quickly filled with weeds and by the following summer it looked like a small jungle, with weeds everywhere.

The interesting thing is that I never saw them in the yard planting weeds. I've never seen anyone plant weeds. Weeds aren't a choice for most homeowners. Weeds are a fact of life in a fallen world. What is a choice is how we deal with weeds. My neighbors decided to give up and let weeds take over. My wife and I have remained diligent to fight weeds and keep our yard healthy. Our backyards were only separated by a fence and we live in the same environment, but our yard looks good.

Sometimes we can identify the source of a sickness, but sometimes we can't. Sometimes it may be something we have "planted" and sometimes it is simply something that appears in our bodies for no discernable reason. It may be a "weed sickness."

Sin in the human race has touched every aspect of our lives. Even our genetic code and our DNA have been impacted by sin. We have all been born with genetic weaknesses or abnormalities. Some need glasses at an early age and some never need glasses. Some have food allergies and some don't. Some have more serious issues from birth and others do not. None of these weakness or challenges were part of God's creation. Their source is Adam's sin. They are the "weeds" that no one planted, but they appear.

How we deal with these physical weakness and sicknesses is up to us. We can sit back and let them rule our lives, or we can decide to be proactive and apply God's grace and Word to the situation.

When Jesus healed the sick, He didn't limit His ministry to diseases. He also healed those who were born with lifelong afflictions.

> *Then great multitudes came to Him, having with them the lame, blind, mute, maimed, and many others; and they laid them down at Jesus' feet, and He healed them* (Matthew 15:30).

In most cases the lame, blind, and mute had been born that way. Those who were maimed refers to those missing limbs! (See Matthew 18:8.)

Whether we are speaking of inherited genetic issues, birth defects, allergies, or heart maladies that aren't discovered until many years later, we are still dealing with things that Jesus bore on the cross. Nothing of the human condition was overlooked in redemption. Everything that Adam's sin unleashed was carried to the cross.

While some of our physical issues may stem from how we have lived our lives, some of them are just "weeds." We didn't plant them. But there is grace to pull them up and out!

Do not lose heart because you were born with a particular physical challenge. All physical issues have the same source—Adam's sin. Jesus fully dealt with the impact of sin in the earth.

> *For as in Adam all die, even so in Christ all shall be made alive* (1 Corinthians 15:22).

All who are born of Adam, which includes me and you, are subject to the consequences of his sin. All who are in Christ can receive the blessings of forgiveness, deliverance, protection, provision, healing, and eternal life with the Father.

We live in a fallen world that is reeling under the weight of sin and death. The environment of this world is programmed for death. Sicknesses are advertised and expected, and drugs with side effects are marketed as the only solution. *But there is a better solution!*

> *His divine power has given to us all things that pertain to life and godliness, through the knowledge of Him who called us by glory and virtue, by which have been given to us exceedingly great and precious promises, that through these you may be partakers of the divine nature, having escaped the corruption that is in the world through lust* (2 Peter 1:3-4).

The Word of God and His promises are His provision for the weeds of life. God's heart is that we *"escape the corruption that is in the world."* We can either see ourselves with authority over weeds, or we can see ourselves letting the weeds take their course. The provision has been given. The weapons of our warfare are mighty in God! (See 2 Corinthians 10:4.)

Regardless of the source of any affliction you may be suffering, God has made provision. Every possible human need was met on the cross. We may suffer persecution for our faith, but we need not suffer sickness and affliction. God's Word is enough. We simply must be convinced and alive to His faith in our hearts.

HEALING PRAYER

Father, I thank You that Your grace has provided for every need in my life. I will walk in Your promises, believe Your Word, and receive Your healing. I will not be passive. I will not allow the weeds of fallen humanity live in my life. I am a new creation, and I choose to walk in Your abundant life! Amen!

Chapter 9

The Attitude of Health and Healing

Our lives are an expression of our attitudes and expectations. How we approach life and the vision we have of ourselves, our environments, and our purpose on this earth are important factors in the type of health we will experience.

FROM THE HEART

*For as he thinks in his **heart**, so is he...* (Proverbs 23:7).

It is from our hearts that we express faith or fear, peace or strife, forgiveness or bitterness, anger or joy. So much of our health is directly tied to the condition of our hearts. When I speak of the heart, I am speaking of the center of our being, the home of our perceived identity, purpose, self-image, and personality.

The heart is the union of our soul and our spirit. With our soul we relate to the world around us and with our spirit we relate to God. Our heart is where we choose whether we will live for the flesh or live for the things of God. How we see ourselves, how we understand God and how we relate to the world around us all flows from our hearts.

> *Keep your **heart** with all diligence, for out of it spring the issues of life* (Proverbs 4:23).

The image we have of ourselves in our hearts is powerful. It is a prophetic picture of the future. Those who see themselves as sick or prone to sickness will reap the harvest of the thoughts of their hearts. Those who see themselves as righteous, healed, and walking in God's grace will have an entirely different experience in life. The image we carry on the inside is the seed of our present and future.

The sick often see themselves as sick, trying to get well. They may accept their sickness as the will of God for some mysterious reason. Healed and healthy people who are challenged with sickness see themselves differently. They are the healed, resisting sickness. They see sickness as an illegal intruder and they choose to resist. The thoughts of their hearts are entirely different, and so are the results.

Think of sickness as a poisonous snake in your house. I once had a friend who found such a snake in his living room, under the couch. His first reaction was not to pray and ask God if the snake was His will. His attitude was not affected at all by theology. The snake presented a very real danger to him and his family, so he killed it. He didn't seek counsel. He didn't seek someone to agree with him in prayer. He didn't buy a book about snakes. He killed the snake. The attitude of his heart had no room for snakes in his house. It was an easy decision.

Until we have God's attitude toward sickness, we will be hindered in possessing our healing. If we believe that the sickness could be of God, or it just runs in the family, or it always happens this time of year, or it just comes with age, then we will accommodate the snake. Many Christians today have allowed the world to shape them after its image, and we have learned to live with snakes—sicknesses.

THE WILL OF GOD

And do not be conformed to this world, but be transformed by the renewing of your mind, that you may prove what is that good and acceptable and perfect will of God (Romans 12:2).

The will of God is good, acceptable, and perfect. It does not include sickness, disease, loss, and suffering. Sadly, the world is striving twenty-four hours a day, seven days a week to conform us to its image. We are constantly bombarded with the idea of sicknesses that have seasons, sicknesses that come with age, sicknesses that are normal in the working world, sicknesses that are normal if you are a man or a woman, etc. Until we truly see all these sicknesses as snakes, we will adjust to them and accept them.

The letter of James speaks of the double-minded being unstable in all their ways (James 1:8). So many Christians are double-minded and many don't even know it. On the one hand they claim to believe in healing, but on the other hand they speak continually of their sickness, their symptoms, what the doctor said, and declare that they hope they get healed if it is His will. This is double-mindedness. The true thoughts of the heart are revealed when we speak. The attitude of such people is resignation, not faith.

Your faith will follow your focus! If you focus on sickness and a negative report, if you meditate on it day and night, and if you speak of it often with any who will listen, you are revealing what is truly in your heart. Your body has no choice but to accept your attitude and your fears.

What constitutes an attitude of health and healing?

> *Finally, brethren, whatever things are true, whatever things are noble, whatever things are just, whatever things are pure, whatever things are lovely, whatever things are of good report, if there is any virtue and if there is anything praiseworthy— meditate on these things* (Philippians 4:8).

This is such a powerful verse and a key to victory in every area of our lives. With regard to the subject of health, I can think of no sickness that is true, noble, just, pure, and lovely. No sickness is worthy of my praise. And yet many Christians are giving praise to the afflictions that attack them by talking about them and meditating on them continually. That attitude will not keep you healthy.

> *A merry heart does good, like medicine, but a broken spirit dries the bones* (Proverbs 17:22).

Remember, out of the heart flow the issues of life! A merry heart is like a medicine. In other words, it is health to your whole being. On the contrary, a broken spirit—sadness of heart, emotional trauma, etc.—can have an opposite effect.

Our attitude has much to do with our health. It creates an environment of faith or fear, hope or despair. Many times it isn't the affliction that is the problem, but rather the attitude that allows the affliction and feeds it. Like Job, many can say, *"For the thing I greatly feared has come upon me, and what I dreaded has happened to me"* (Job 3:25).

Your focus in life will be either positive or negative. That focus creates an attitude and that attitude can allow sickness or hinder healing.

In 1978, my wife experienced severe complications and blood loss from a pregnancy. I rushed her to a doctor who performed various tests and examinations. The following day I returned to the doctor for the results while my wife rested at home in bed. The doctor showed me the sonogram results on a screen and proclaimed, "The fetus is dead." Something from deep inside of me cried out, "No!" Looking back now I understand that I had an attitude of expectancy, of life and of health. It was a foundational motivation that was "attacked" by the doctor's proclamation. Had my attitude been one of "whatever will be, will be," or some other passive approach to the moment, I doubt we would have seen the miracle that happened.

When I returned home, my wife asked what the doctor said. I chose to quote Dr. Jesus and not the doctor I had just visited. I told her to just rest and everything would be OK. I had an attitude of victory. I wasn't willing to adjust my attitude to conform to the doctor's declaration of death. The Spirit of God had been stirred within and my "No" was not just an emotion, but a declaration of what the Spirit had quickened to my heart.

Sometimes "no" is the most powerful word the Spirit will put in your heart. No to fear, no to sickness, no to poverty, no to depression, and no to the influence of the world!

Our son, David, was born two weeks late, but perfectly healthy and normal. We didn't return to the doctor we first visited. My attitude wasn't in agreement with his. My vision for my child was life, not death.

You can be of quiet demeanor, which I am, but aggressive in your attitude. Just as you wouldn't knowingly let someone burglarize your home, you shouldn't allow sickness to steal your life. How we see our value to God establishes an attitude. How we understand our purpose in life establishes an attitude. How we value the promises of God, our family, and our future establishes an attitude. You don't have to be rude to have an attitude! You simply must be committed to believing God's Word and actively pursuing Him. Health and long life are His gifts to you. What is your attitude toward His provision?

One of the perks of working in my position in Charis Bible College is that I am assigned a parking spot. It's my parking spot. No one else should park there. When I arrive to work or to an event and I find someone else's car in my parking spot, I might be agitated. I have been known to leave a note on the windshield of the offending driver.

Healing has been "assigned" to you. But you may need the right attitude to keep sickness from parking in your life.

You may need to remind your body and the enemy that they aren't allowed in your spot. You may have to get aggressive. Is healing your right, or not? It definitely is as a child of God!

HEALING PRAYER

Father, I choose to have Your attitude of health and healing in my heart. I choose to see my life free from sickness. I choose victory, the joy of the Lord, and abundant life, in Jesus' name! Amen!

Chapter 10

What Do You Expect?

Our attitude is very similar to our foundational expectations in life. The subject of health must include a discussion of our expectations. Expectations are powerful. We all have them whether they are spoken or unspoken.

> *According to my earnest expectation and hope...*
> (Philippians 1:20).

I received a tremendous revelation about this topic a few years ago. I noticed in Philippians 1:20 that Paul distinguished between expectation and hope. I was intrigued. As I studied the definitions of the words, I felt a new understanding dawning upon me.

An expectation can be defined as intense anticipation. It isn't necessarily positive or negative. It can be either an intense anticipation of good or of evil. Hope can be defined as a positive expectation. In other words, an intense anticipation, an expectation, can be positive or negative. Hope is the positive, intense anticipation of good. Some live their lives always expecting the worst. A pessimist has perpetual negative expectations. As someone once said, "A pessimist is always disappointed in the future!"

Some are raised in environments of negative expectations and fears. Expecting whatever can go wrong to go wrong is a conscious or subconscious approach to life that creates an environment that will harvest what is expected.

It is interesting that we all live in one realm or the other. We are either positive in our outlook on life, or we are negative. That outlook is an expectation. Some expect to be sick, to be poor, to be the first fired, and to have persistent problems and chronic failure in life. But some of these same people will go to church and easily proclaim, "I'm believing God for my healing!" No. They are not. They can't.

> *Now faith is the substance of things hoped for, the evidence of things not seen* (Hebrews 11:1).

If faith is the substance of hope, and hope is a positive, intense anticipation of good, then it is impossible to be in faith with a negative expectation as the foundation of your life! If the expectation in life is negative, it is like trying to grow crops in salted soil. Nothing will grow if the soil is contaminated. Faith cannot flow from the soil of negative expectations! That is why the thoughts of our hearts are so important. As we think in our hearts—expectations, image, faith, purpose—so are we! (See Proverbs 23:7.)

Your view of life, of God and of yourself carries a subconscious or conscious expectation. That expectation will either suffocate faith or allow it to prosper. This is incredibly important. You cannot believe for healing if you are simultaneously expecting to live a life of failure, sickness, and defeat.

I have ministered to many who want to be sure that I understand every aspect of their affliction and how bad it is. They can quote the names and initials of all their maladies, tell me the doctor's diagnosis, the drugs they are taking, and the side effects. Their hearts are filled to overflowing with information about their sickness. And then they want me to pray for them and agree with them for their healing. Do you see a problem? I do. Out of the abundance of the heart the mouth speaks (Matthew 12:34), and the heart is the factory of expectation (Matthew 12:35). I would be much more motivated to agree with them in prayer if I heard any faith coming from their hearts.

POSITIVE EXPECTATIONS

Where do positive expectations come from? They are most certainly a result of renewing the mind to God's will, that which is good, acceptable, and perfect.

> And **do not be conformed to this world**, but be **transformed by the renewing of your mind**, that you may prove what is that **good and acceptable and perfect will of God** (Romans 12:2).

The more we meditate on God's promises and understand that He has made us worthy to receive all His grace, we can begin to reshape our expectations on the Word of God and not on our fears and experiences of the world or from the past.

If we see ourselves as unworthy, we will expect to be treated as unworthy. There may be some crumbs of blessings that fall from God's table from time to time, but we see ourselves under the table. We will have an "under the table" expectation in life.

But when we get a revelation of the gift of righteousness (Romans 5:17), our expectations change. I'm not worthy because of what I've done or haven't done. I'm worthy because of what Jesus accomplished on my behalf. My right to be healed is not based upon my worthiness, but upon His worthiness! This is mind-boggling and hard for many to comprehend, but it is true. This is where a positive expectation is born. I expect to walk in health because of Jesus.

God is the God of hope. He is the Giver of good gifts. Spend time in His promises and feed your heart with His love and desire for your life. You can either have an attitude of resignation, fear, and sadness, or you can stand on God's Word and have an attitude of positive expectation and hope. It is then that faith can spring forth to receive the grace of healing.

Everyone who sought out Jesus did so because they were expecting to be healed. Only one man asked Jesus if it was His will to heal (Mark 1:40-41). That pattern holds true today. A positive expectation is the birthplace of miracles!

A positive expectation is based upon a promise and the accompanying vision of that promise being fulfilled. As a child, if my parents promised a trip to an amusement park or the beach, an expectation was created and imaginations followed quickly. I could see myself riding a roller coaster or swimming in the waves. I had no doubt that the promise would be fulfilled. My parents had spoken.

Faith is the substance of things hoped for. My hope was based upon a promise from my parents. My positive expectation gave birth to preparations. I would tell my friends of my upcoming adventure. I would check my clothes to make sure I had what I needed. I would ask my mom about what we would eat. I was fully prepared to enjoy the future based upon a promise! Words changed me. Words gave birth to hope, and from hope came faith.

FAITH FOR HEALING

Faith for healing is nothing more than the excitement over a promise from the Father. Promises create expectations, hope, and a vision for the future. When we build our lives on His promises and fill our hearts with His Word, we have created the atmosphere for His will to come to pass.

What do you expect for the rest of your life? What do you expect for your health? What words have filled your heart and created your expectations? What do you expect for your marriage, your children, or your job or ministry?

As you look at your future, the power of expectation is at work for you or against you. Your health can be an outcome of your attitude and expectation. If you expect to be sick, to grow old and experience age-related issues as described on TV, then that is what you will harvest. You are attracting what you expect!

When we allow the Word of God to shape and form our expectations, an attitude will develop. We won't accept the words of death, defeat, and failure. We will respond as Jesus did with, *"It is written!"*

*Your words were found, and I ate them, and Your
word was to me the joy and rejoicing of my heart...*
(Jeremiah 15:16).

Victorious, overcoming Christians expect to be victorious, overcoming Christians! Their attitude is positive, and their vision sees beyond the temporal into the eternal. Expectation is an actual force that attracts according to its nature. A negative expectation will attract negative life events. A positive expectation will attract blessings. A positive expectation is the environment of the God kind of faith!

Our bodies recognize the condition of our hearts. Just as our bodies respond to what we feed them, they also respond to our expectations, vision, words, and faith. Things in the world of the spirit will line up with the expectation we are manifesting, either of good or evil, life or death.

*According to my earnest expectation and hope that
in nothing I shall be ashamed* (Philippians 1:20).

Expect health and healing. Expect long life. Expect to finish your course and accomplish God's purpose for your life. There is grace for you! Align yourself with His grace and kill the snake!

HEALING PRAYER

*Father, today I choose to accept how You have valued
me and given me Your righteousness. As Your child,
I expect Your blessings, Your grace, and Your health
in my life. I expect the abundant life! Amen!*

Chapter 11

Releasing Healing

We must come to know what it means to have Jesus, the Father, the Holy Spirit living within us. We have been transformed by the Spirit of God and we are one spirit with Him.

> *But he who is joined to the Lord is one spirit with Him* (1 Corinthians 6:17).

A revelation of the Greater One living within should have a great impact on our expectations and attitude toward life. We are seated with Him in heavenly places in the Spirit (Ephesians 2:6). We have been called to reign in life!

> *For if by the one man's* [Adam] *offense death reigned through the one, much more those who receive abundance of grace and of the gift of righteousness will reign in life through the One, Jesus Christ* (Romans 5:17).

If Jesus lives within us by the Spirit, then all that He is, is within us. His life and nature are in us and that would include health and healing. Because the Creator and Sustainer of life lives within, then our healing lives within!

I have been attacked with symptoms of pain, discomfort, or other issues from time to time. Like anyone else, I can let myself imagine that the symptom as a sign of some serious ailment or disease. I can allow fear in my heart. I can look up the symptom on the Internet and imagine how terrible this might be. If I let myself, I could calculate how long I had left to live!

But thank God, I have a different foundation in my life! When a symptom presents itself, I immediately decide that it has no place in my body or my life. I get aggressive against it, declare the Word of God over it, and keep on going.

A few years ago, I was bothered by something out of place in my foot which made it painful to walk. Unconsciously, I adjusted to a different way to walk to minimize the pain. I assumed the pain would leave soon, but in the meantime I adjusted. This went on for a few weeks. During a ministry trip, I found myself traveling through three airports over four days and doing a lot of walking. My foot was hurting more and more and my weight distribution on my foot was becoming so different that it was apparent to those around that I was in pain or slightly disabled.

In the midst of one long walk to a terminal gate, I stopped. I thought to myself, *This isn't right. This shouldn't be happening.* And then I declared, "I am going to walk normally no matter how much it hurts! I am going to beat this right now!" I took a step and my foot screamed with pain. I took another step and the pain was still there. When I took the third step, the pain instantly disappeared! I have never had that issue again! I decided to take authority and release the healing power of God over that situation. I decided to "reign" over that situation rather than be passive and accepting.

Our God is the God of faith. The faith of God does not fail. The faith of God inside us is a healing faith. It is part of our reborn spiritual nature. Everything that Jesus was in His earthly ministry He now is within us! The power of God lives within the believer.

> *Now to Him who is able to do exceedingly abundantly above all that we ask or think, **according to the power that works in us*** (Ephesians 3:20).

Most Christians see healing as coming from outside of them, probably from above. They see themselves as sick trying to get well. They pray and ask and hope that something outside of them will touch them.

Of course, when Jesus walked the earth and healed all who came to Him, He was indeed outside of the sick and healed them from the outside. But now He lives within us, and His healing power is within us! This is a thought that is hard for some to grasp. We have been so indoctrinated to believe that we must convince God to heal us, or that we must find an anointed minister to bring healing to us, that we have completely neglected the reality of Who lives within. Because the Spirit of Almighty God lives within me, then all of the healing I need is within me!

In our spirit, the law of sin and death has been defeated. We are new creations. The law of the Spirit of life in Christ Jesus is our new reality. Healing is within us! So few believe or even want to believe this truth. Rather than releasing the healing within, many have created theologies of excuses that steal the believer's inheritance in Christ.

Our attitude, vision, and expectations will focus on how we understand the problem, the sickness, and how we perceive the answer could come—healing. When we limit healing to a supernatural event that comes from "up there," we are neglecting the very real truth that Jesus lives within us. Why can't healing come from "in there"? Are we not the temple of the Holy Spirit?

> *Or do you not know that your body is the temple of the Holy Spirit who is in you, whom you have from God, and you are not your own?* (1 Corinthians 6:19)

When we deal with sickness in our own bodies, we must see ourselves as the healed resisting sickness, rather than the sick trying to get healed. Sickness is an illegal intruder that must be expelled from our bodies. We can speak to our bodies by the Spirit. The physical must submit to the spiritual. The visible must submit to the invisible.

In the case of my hurting foot, the answer came quickly, once I decided I had had enough. In other cases I will speak of later, I had to stand fast in my expectation and declaration. By faith and patience we inherit the promises (Hebrews 6:12).

FAITH'S REALITY

All the healing we need is available through our reborn spirits that are one with God. Healing can come from within. It comes from the same place that righteousness comes from.

It is faith's reality. We release it with our words, our attitudes, our thoughts, and actions. We act on the Word, speak the Word, think the Word, and "see" the healing with our spiritual eyes. The body will conform to the image of God that we carry on the inside. If we're OK with snakes in the house, snakes will live there.

We don't need to ask God if it is His will to heal us. His will was for His presence to dwell in us. When He came to live in you, He didn't bring everything with Him except healing. Healing is part of His name! *"I am the Lord who heals you,"* is living in you! (See Exodus 15:26.) We really don't need to be limited to seeking healing or hoping for healing. It can simply be a matter of us releasing the healing of God who lives within.

Just as we choose to release His love, His patience, His kindness, and His faithfulness, we can choose to release His healing. We choose to be kind or generous because that is the fruit of the Spirit, and those motivations are of God and are permanently present within. So is health. I can't imagine a theological scenario in which God lives within us, but His power for healing didn't make the trip with Him. Didn't Jesus command us to lay hands on the sick and they would recover? Where is that power coming from? It comes from Jehovah Rapha Himself who lives within us!

We can choose health just as we can choose to forgive others. There are no limits other than the ones we allow.

> *Now to Him who is able to do exceedingly abundantly above all that we ask or think, **according to the power that works in us*** (Ephesians 3:20).

That verse deserves some meditation! When we have a clear understanding and revelation that the Healer lives within—the power that works in us—we are on the way to seeing the manifestation of healing. If you can see it with the eyes of faith, you can receive it.

HEALING PRAYER

Father, I receive the revelation of Your presence in my life. You are the Greater One who lives within, and Your power to heal is within me. I release Your healing power into every part of my being and I believe that Your Spirit is making me alive! Amen!

Chapter 12

The Power of Words

In 2001, after over twelve years on the mission field, the Lord was leading us to return to Texas. We had sold or given away our possessions and we were going to return to the United States in much the same way we had arrived in Chile—with two suitcases per person.

The one thing I had failed to sell was my car. The car had been a blessing during our last few years in Santiago and I had put it up for sale, but there were no offers. As I remember, it was a Thursday morning and we were due to fly out on Saturday. I was reading my Bible and praying, mostly about the car, when I came to Romans 4:17:

> ...*God, who gives life to the dead and calls those things which do not exist as though they did.*

When my eyes fell on those words, I heard the Spirit of God say to me, "That's how I do it." My first response was, "Yes, I teach that." Then I realized that I had just heard from God! The Spirit had quickened a truth to my spirit and I jumped out of my chair and declared, "I call this car sold TODAY in Jesus' name!"

Something inside of me was stirred. Faith was born. Words were spoken. The world of the Spirit was in motion!

I had some banking to attend to in town with my assistant pastor, so I drove the car to the appointment. While inside the bank, my cell phone rang. A man was outside, had seen the "For Sale" sign in the window of the car, and was interested. I told him to come into the bank and when I was finished with business, we could talk.

A few minutes later, I was giving him a ride around the block in my car. He asked what the price was and when I told him he immediately said, "I'll take it." I asked how we could make the deal and he said that his bank was across the street. We made a transfer of funds, visited a notary half a block away, and the deal was done. Literally two hours from hearing from God and declaring that which was quickened to my spirit, I was taking my personal belongings out of the car and handing the new owner the keys!

Words are the most powerful force in the universe. God created all things with words. He spoke, and from the invisible world of the Spirit, our tangible, visible universe came forth.

> *By faith we understand that the worlds were framed by the word of God, so that the things which are seen were not made of things which are visible* (Hebrews 11:3).

We must understand the beginning of all things if we are going to tap into the infinite power of God's Word for health and healing. How did God bring forth the visible from the invisible?

> ...*God, who gives life to the dead and calls those things which do not exist as though they did* (Romans 4:17).

THE INVISIBLE BECOMES VISIBLE

When God said, *"Let there be..."* in Genesis 1, what was invisible became visible and tangible according to the vision, design, and purpose of the Creator. The Word declares that He now upholds all things by the word of His power.

> *Who being the brightness of His glory and the express image of His person, and upholding all things by the word of His power...* (Hebrews 1:3).

Everything that we can see and touch is a physical substance that was created by and is sustained by the Word of God. The visible is proof of the invisible and is only visible because God declared it!

While this may be hard for our human minds to grasp, it is a vital truth that we must consider when we speak of healing. The visible is subject to the invisible. The material world is subject to the spiritual world. Our bodies are subject to God's Word.

Words are vibrations of sound that have a source and a purpose. God's Words are divine vibrations with a divine source and purpose.

...I am ready to perform My word (Jeremiah 1:12).

So shall My word be that goes forth from My mouth; it shall not return to Me void, but it shall accomplish what I please, and it shall prosper in the thing for which I sent it (Isaiah 55:11).

When the Creator of the universe speaks, life and purpose are in His words! His words will accomplish their purpose. The amazing thing for believers is that we were created with the same potential! God has given us the authority to see the invisible and speak it into reality. As long as we are in agreement with His Word and His nature, our words release the power of His Word.

For assuredly, I say to you, whoever says to this mountain, "Be removed and be cast into the sea," and does not doubt in his heart, but believes that those things he says will be done, he will have whatever he says (Mark 11:23).

This is an incredible promise with which many have struggled. Certainly, it can't mean what it says! But it means exactly what it says. God created man in His image and man has the authority to speak God's words. Even though sin corrupted that privilege and authority for thousands of years, Jesus has redeemed it for His church. Life-giving words are once again available to heal the sick and establish God's will in our lives.

A man's stomach shall be satisfied from the fruit of his mouth; from the produce of his lips he shall be filled. Death and life are in the power of the tongue, and those who love it will eat its fruit (Proverbs 18:20-21).

LIFE AND DEATH ARE IN THE TONGUE

Death and life are in the power of the tongue! The subject of words has now become very relevant to our study of healing. The words we speak establish death or life in our lives. The results may not be instantaneous, but our words give authority to spiritual forces to bring those words to pass. We are either speaking in agreement with God and His words, or we are speaking the language of darkness, corruption, and sickness.

> *For out of the abundance of the heart the mouth speaks. A good man out of the good treasure of his heart brings forth good things, and an evil man out of the evil treasure brings forth evil things* (Matthew 12:34-35).

In our context of healing, the heart will speak according to our vision and expectations concerning our health. We will either be speaking life or death, faith or fear, and those words carry power.

Words are like seeds. Seeds have a source. The words we speak have a source. The source determines the nature of the seeds and the nature of the words. A watermelon will produce watermelon seeds. The seeds bear the nature of a watermelon. Our hearts are the source of our words and our words will bear the nature of our hearts. A heart of fear and doubt will sow "word seeds" of death.

Remember, death and life are in the power of the tongue! A heart filled with faith in God's Word will speak God's words. Words filled with God's Word and His promises carry God's life and authority. When we couple this truth with the earlier discussion of our attitude and expectations, we can understand that our words reveal both our attitudes and expectations.

Our words have the capacity to make alive or kill. Words of condemnation, criticism, hopelessness, and fear spoken to a child can shape their life toward loss and failure. Words of love, peace, grace, and encouragement will have the opposite effect.

Consider the story of Jairus again. Jairus had gone to Jesus on behalf of his daughter who was at the point of death. Jesus agreed to go to the home of Jairus to heal her. Jairus' initial declaration was that if Jesus would simply lay His hands on his daughter, she would live. As they approached the home, friends came from Jairus' house to tell him it was too late.

> *While He was still speaking, some came from the ruler of the synagogue's house who said, "Your daughter is dead. Why trouble the Teacher any further?" As soon as Jesus heard the word that was spoken, He said to the ruler of the synagogue, "Do not be afraid; only believe"* (Mark 5:35-36).

What was Jesus concerned about? *"Do not be afraid, only believe."* How would Jesus detect fear in Jairus? By his words. If Jairus cried out in anguish and blamed himself, or blamed Jesus, or blamed other circumstances, his words would have over-whelmed his initial declaration. That is why Jesus cautioned Jairus, *"Do not be afraid, only believe."* In other words, don't open your mouth! Don't mess this up with unbelief and grief.

Sometimes, the best thing to say is nothing at all. Until we have the mind of the Lord and words of faith and life, it would be better to keep silent.

When we take this truth into the realm of our own health challenges, how many of us are still speaking words of death, doubt, and fear? Have we realized how much negative power we are releasing into the situation? Making sure everyone knows every detail of the sickness, every word the doctor said, and every possible scenario for the future of the disease is not life to you or anyone around you. Death and life are in the power of the tongue! That is why Jesus declared,

> *"It is written, 'Man shall not live by bread alone,*
> *but by every word that proceeds from the mouth of*
> *God'"* (Matthew 4:4).

Only His words carry His life and authority. The words we speak are either birthed in fear and doubt or come from the Spirit of God. That is why Jesus only spoke what He heard the Father speaking.

> *...the word which you hear is not Mine but the*
> *Father's who sent Me* (John 14:24).

Can you imagine what your life could be like if you only spoke words that are born of the Spirit and the life-giving words of the Scriptures?

SPEAK LIFE-GIVING WORDS

Scientific tests have been conducted for decades that demonstrate the power of positive words and negative words on plants and other forms of life. The most common tests occur with plants or fruits that are subjected to negative words while other identical plants and fruits are subjected to positive words. In every case I have seen, the plants and fruits subjected to negative words suffered quick withering and death or corruption, while the fruits and plants that were subjected to life-giving words of love, joy, peace, and abundance all fared much better.

Can plants understand words? Not as you and I do, but human words carry the nature of their source. Words in any language bear the nature and the attitude of the heart from which they spring. When our hearts are filled with anxiety, fear and doubt, or bitterness and anger, those words release their nature into the circumstances. Out of the abundance of the heart the mouth speaks, and death or life go to work!

> *...For out of the abundance of the heart the mouth speaks. A good man out of the good treasure of his heart brings forth good things, and an evil man out of the evil treasure brings forth evil things* (Matthew 12:34-35).

If even plants can respond to this power, what can we expect if God's Word fills our hearts?

> *So the Lord said, "If you have faith as a mustard seed, you can say to this mulberry tree, 'Be pulled*

up by the roots and be planted in the sea,' and it would obey you" (Luke 17:6).

A tree will obey faith-filled words! What about a sickness?

*My son, give attention to **my words**; incline your ear to my sayings. Do not let them depart from your eyes; keep them in the midst of your heart; for they **are life** to those who find them, **and health** to all their flesh* (Proverbs 4:20-22).

This does not mean simply acknowledging the power of words and moving on. The secret of everything we are speaking of is in these verses. Look closely and consider this exhortation.

- Give attention to His words. Giving attention implies perseverance and dedication.

- Incline your ear to His sayings. Inclining the ear speaks of focus. You don't want to miss anything!

- Do not let them depart from your eyes. Keep the Word of God in front of you and let no worthless thing distract you.

- Keep them in the midst of your heart. Meditate on His Word day and night. Why? His words are life and health.

Your heart is the source of your faith, vision, and future! The Word of God is a fountain of life and health! It will fulfill its purpose when it finds an environment in which it can prosper. Can God's Word prosper in your heart?

He sent His word and healed them, and delivered them from their destructions (Psalm 107:20).

HEALING PRAYER

Father, I will fill my heart with Your words. I will speak words of life and health. Life is in the power of my tongue, and I will release Your life into my circumstances. Amen!

Chapter 13

What Is Faith?

Jesus said to him, "If you can believe, all things are possible to him who believes" (Mark 9:23).

The subject of faith has led to much misunderstanding and discouragement. When we fail to understand faith, the tendency is to blame God for our challenges. Entire theologies have risen to explain away the promises of faith found in the Bible. Many will proclaim their great faith but see no results in their bodies. Such experiences lead to belief systems that allow for sickness and teach people to accept the seeds of doubt. Others have redefined faith to look exactly like resignation. When we declare that God has a purpose in everything and we should just trust Him, it can sound like faith, but in reality it is fate.

As I shared at the beginning of this book, while in Guatemala I became aware of the difference between what I know in my head and what has been revealed to my heart. Something transpired in my heart that transformed Bible knowledge into revelation knowledge. The best way to describe it would be in this verse:

The Spirit Himself bears witness with our spirit...
(Romans 8:16).

Something I knew and believed in my head instantly became alive in my spirit. And that is when faith came!

What I had known in my head I now knew in my heart! I thought I had been in faith, but I instantly knew the difference. The quickening of the Spirit of God's declaration to my spirit (*"by His stripes we are healed";* Isaiah 53:5) gave birth to true faith! In that instant I knew I was healed. Faith had come by hearing God.

So then faith comes by hearing, and hearing by the word of God (Romans 10:17).

I have learned in subsequent years that this "quickening" or "hearing" can come instantly or over time. It isn't that God is withholding His Word from me, but rather that I need to come to a place of "tuning in" to His frequency. His Word is always alive and active, but we often are distracted or too worried to hear Him.

Faith is not mental. It is spiritual. Faith is of the heart.

For with the heart one believes... (Romans 10:10).

Knowledge about faith is not faith. Having testimonies of faith in the past is not necessarily faith for the present. Faith has but one source—hearing God.

UNDERSTANDING FAITH'S SOURCE

We were created to hear God. We were created to live in communion with Him. We are created to live by hearing Him! What is the result of hearing God? Faith!

Jesus answered, "It is written: 'Man shall not live by bread alone, but by every word that proceeds from the mouth of God'" (Matthew 4:4).

Faith is easy when you understand its source. If faith comes by hearing God, then faith should be the normal condition of every Christian! Jesus said, *"My sheep hear My voice"* (John 10:27). Sadly, many never enter into this kind of relationship with the Father. When hard times or physical afflictions come, they are unprepared. Mental belief about healing becomes a struggle of knowledge and willpower. Frustration ensues and doubts arise. As a result, many adopt theologies that accept and even defend sickness as God's mysterious will.

How often I have had people come to me for prayer for healing, and when I asked what God had spoken or what promise had been quickened to them, I would be met with a blank stare. Many Christians simply do not live with even a minimal relationship with the Father in which they expect to hear Him. There is grace for them. God is merciful to our weaknesses. But so much more is possible!

The key to receiving from God is to hear God. The more we hear, the more we will live by faith. We will see the unseen and speak words that give life.

Now faith is the substance of things hoped for, the evidence of things not seen (Hebrews 11:1).

There are two aspects of this first verse in Hebrews 11 I want to consider. First, we have already discussed the power of expectation and hope. Until there is positive expectation for your life based upon the promises of God, it will be difficult to walk in true faith. Faith is the substance of an intense, positive expectation that comes only from the quickening power of God's Word to your spirit. Faith is not simply knowledge! Again, knowledge about faith is not faith. Faith is spiritual and comes from a spiritual interaction with God.

Second, faith takes us into the realm of the "unseen." This is where many falter. They won't "believe" until the answer is obvious to their senses. That is not faith. Faith is not sense related. It is Word related. It is spiritual, not mental.

If I have a dog and have trained the dog to obey my commands, I have certainty that when I give a command, the dog will obey. If I own a business and I give a command to a worker, I have certainty that the worker will follow the instruction. There is no doubt in my heart about dogs or workers over which I have authority.

However, if I give an order to a strange dog or to a person who doesn't work for me, I must wait to "see" what will happen. I have left the realm of faith and I am now walking by sight! Please meditate on this. When dealing with a strange dog, because authority has not been established, I must judge the effect of my words by what I see.

In such cases, the strange dog holds the power. My confidence is not related to the authority of my words, but now must depend on the actions of a dog. That is not faith! I may "believe" that I have authority over a dog I don't know, and I may feel I spoke with "authority," but I am at the mercy of the dog's response. This is the reality of many believers in the realm of healing.

Most believers walk by sight, not by faith. Their faith is mental, and their expectation is based upon what they see and feel. Once they feel better, they will "believe" they are healed. If the strange dog obeys, they will breathe a sigh of relief. But they don't know what will happen before it happens, only after. That is not faith!

FAITH KNOWS THE OUTCOME

If you don't know what will happen before it happens, you are walking by sight, not by faith. Faith knows the outcome before it comes out! Anything that traps you in the realm of your senses will have dominion over you. If sickness can keep you in the sense realm, it can destroy you; but *if you deal with sickness from the faith realm, you will destroy it.*

Let me be clear that we aren't talking about a lack of faith. If you had faith to be born again, you have faith to be healed. You have all the faith you need. The issue is the activation of faith. It can be compared to having a treasure chest in your possession filled with every kind of jewel, gold, silver, and money. However, if you don't have the key, the treasure remains locked away.

Hearing God is the key to activation. Hearing can happen in a number of ways, but it refers to something of the Spirit being revealed to us on the spiritual level. All believers have faith. If we are born again, we have the God kind of faith within.

When the Spirit quickens His truths to your spirit, your faith is activated. Whether we say faith is born, or faith is conceived, or faith comes, matters not. Let's just say that hearing God activates the God kind of faith. "Hearing" can be the quickening of a verse, a "light bulb" moment that sets you free, or a surge of divine compassion while praying. Hearing Him can take on many forms, but you will know you have heard Him when faith arises in your heart and words and actions spring forth.

Faith is the great equalizer among people. It is available to the rich, the poor, the mighty, the weak, the winners, and the losers in life. Everything in God's provision of grace is available to anyone who can believe. All are equal in the eyes of God, and all can believe and receive. God's Word is always alive and active and yes and amen.

Faith can be compared to electricity in a house. The house is wired and the power is on, but if I don't know how to plug in an appliance, I will never get the benefit. If I call the power company and they then instruct me over the phone as to how to plug in, I will have all the power I need. The phone call simply made me aware of what already existed. The person on the other end of the phone wasn't sovereignly deciding if I deserved electricity, and wasn't flipping the switch on a whim. The power is in the house. The problem was a lack of "revelation" knowledge.

Faith connects the time-related needs of the present with eternity where every need is met.

> *And when He had come into the house, the blind men came to Him. And Jesus said to them, "**Do you believe** that I am able to do this?" They said to Him, "Yes, Lord." Then He touched their eyes, saying, "According to **your faith** let it be to you." And their eyes were opened...* (Matthew 9:28-30).

It is interesting that Jesus put the burden of healing on the two blind men and not on Himself. So often we expect God to swoop down and heal us, when in fact, all we need is the faith to access His grace. He said, *"According to **your** faith let it be to you."* This is significant.

GOD KIND OF FAITH DOESN'T FAIL

I am very aware that some who will read this may think, *I know I have faith! Why am I not healed?* If that is you, I don't want to argue with your declaration, but I would suggest that the God kind of faith doesn't fail. Perhaps we have confused knowledge about God's goodness and knowledge about faith with true faith.

While our personal faith is important, thankfully, it isn't the only way to be healed. We will discuss other methods of healing later. It remains important for us, however, to understand the power of faith and where true faith comes from. Until we understand faith, we may struggle in our own strength to "work it up."

Faith is the revelation of the will of God to the human spirit, which produces certainty, conviction, and action. When the God kind of faith is stirred within, no one needs to tell you what to say or what to do. You no longer ask for everyone's opinion. You no longer go from prayer line to prayer line. You don't need to be encouraged by others. You have heard from God and you know that you know! The declaration of words of life will flow. The vision of health will overwhelm you. The action of faith will be normal and easy. This is the difference between trying to work up faith mentally, and simply hearing from God.

Hearing from God is probably the greatest need in the body of Christ today. Jesus could do nothing except what He heard and saw the Father do. Why do we think we can get better results with a lesser relationship with the Father? Jesus said:

> *I speak what I have seen with My Father...* (John 8:38).

> *Most assuredly, I say to you, the Son can do nothing of Himself, but what He sees the Father do...* (John 5:19).

Faith is easy when we understand how it is activated.

> *So then faith comes by hearing, and hearing by the word of God* (Romans 10:17).

Expect to hear from God every day. Expect a revelation, a confirmation, or an idea that solves a problem. Expect a verse to come alive. Expect wisdom, a new peace, or a burst of inspiration. As you spend time in the Word and prayer, you should grow in sensitivity to the Holy Spirit. This relationship will become your Source of knowledge, wisdom, revelation, and faith. You were created for this!

HEALING PRAYER

Father, I thank You that I am hearing Your living Word and faith is coming alive within! Amen!

Chapter 14

Kinds of Faith

When we speak of faith, it is good to consider three different expressions of faith: proactive; inactive; and reactive.

Proactive faith is the faith that pursues and possesses the answer based upon hearing the Word. The woman with the issue of blood had proactive faith. The man on the cot and his four friends who opened a hole in a roof had proactive faith. Anyone who heard of Jesus and went out to where He was had proactive faith. They pursued Jesus based upon the revelation of His nature, character, and power. They did not sit at home.

It is interesting that while multitudes sought after Jesus, many more did not. In John chapter 5, we find the story of the man lame for thirty-eight years, lying by the pool of Bethesda.

> *Now there is in Jerusalem by the Sheep Gate a pool, which is called in Hebrew, Bethesda, having five porches. In these lay a great multitude of sick people, blind, lame, paralyzed, waiting for the moving of the water* (John 5:2-3).

No doubt this great multitude had heard of Jesus, but they were content to remain by the pool.

> *Then His fame went throughout all Syria; and they brought to Him all sick people who were afflicted with various diseases and torments, and those who were demon-possessed, epileptics, and paralytics; and He healed them* (Matthew 4:24).

It is interesting that though His healing ministry was known throughout the land, a great multitude chose to stay by a pool of water in which supposedly only one person would be healed *if* the waters were stirred.

It is my personal opinion that the stirring of the waters by an angel was a myth. I can find nothing in the Law of the Old Testament that indicates that God would heal His people in that way. One source I read believes this place and tradition came from Greek mythology and was not related to the Jews at all.

Regardless, God sent Jesus to heal His people and this multitude was not seeking Jesus. They did not have proactive faith based upon a revelation of Jesus' nature and power. No revelation, no faith. Belief in what could have been a superstition was more important to this group. Many are held captive to superstitions and religious thinking in our day as well. I refer to this as inactive faith.

Inactive faith suggests that faith is present but has not been activated by a revelation or word from God. It is the idea that if God wants to heal me, He knows where I live. It is passive resignation. It can be identified by the statement, "I'm just waiting for my healing to manifest." In other words, "When my body tells me I'm healed, I'll know I'm healed." Inactive faith is tied to the senses, not to the Word.

The third expression of faith I refer to is *reactive faith*. Reactive faith is a spontaneous reaction to hearing the Word. Unexpectedly one will hear a truth from the gospel and instantly respond and receive from God.

> *And in Lystra a certain man without strength in his feet was sitting, a cripple from his mother's womb, who had never walked. This man heard Paul speaking. Paul, observing him intently and seeing that he had faith to be healed, said with a loud voice, "Stand up straight on your feet!" And he leaped and walked* (Acts 14:8-10).

The man at Lystra just happened to be where Paul stopped to preach. He was not planning to get healed that day. There was no declaration of faith such as we find in the story of the woman with the issue of blood. This man happened to be in the right place at the right time. He heard Paul share the gospel and faith was activated. Paul could see the man's countenance change. Something had happened. His spirit had reacted to the Word and faith came alive.

Reactive faith can happen anytime the Word is shared. The Holy Spirit can use the environment of preaching and teaching to fill the open heart of the listener. Of course, a hardened heart will not receive the Word. But the man at Lystra did hear and was instantly healed.

WHAT ABOUT UNBELIEF?

Just as faith can be a reactive awakening to hearing the Word of God, unbelief can creep subtly into the heart and stop the flow of God's grace. Jesus ran into unbelief in His own hometown.

> *Now He could do no mighty work there, except that He laid His hands on a few sick people and healed them. And He marveled because of their unbelief. Then He went about the villages in a circuit, teaching* (Mark 6:5-6).

While a few sick people were receptive to Jesus, the majority were not. Their unbelief stopped the mighty works that Jesus would have done in their midst. This is a sobering thought. How many miracles have we missed because we were in an environment of unbelief? When intellect, logic, and doubt are allowed to reign, faith in the unseen will disappear.

Unbelief is a sensitive subject for most of us. Because we have confused knowledge with faith—knowledge is of the head and is mental, while faith is of the heart and is spiritual—I doubt we realize how often we are in unbelief.

> *And when they had come to the multitude, a man came to Him, kneeling down to Him and saying, "Lord, have mercy on my son, for he is an epileptic and suffers severely; for he often falls into the fire and often into the water. So I brought him to Your disciples, but they could not cure him." Then Jesus answered and said, "O faithless and perverse*

generation, how long shall I be with you? How long shall I bear with you? Bring him here to Me." And Jesus rebuked the demon, and it came out of him; and the child was cured from that very hour. Then the disciples came to Jesus privately and said, "Why could we not cast it out?" So Jesus said to them, "Because of your unbelief; for assuredly, I say to you, if you have faith as a mustard seed, you will say to this mountain, 'Move from here to there,' and it will move; and nothing will be impossible for you" (Matthew 17:14-20).

In this well-known story, a father brings his tormented child to the disciples and they could not deliver him. This is interesting because these same disciples had already been commissioned to heal the sick and cast out demons and had undoubtedly done so in other cases. Yet in this case they were ineffective.

In the modern theological framework of many churches this would have been understood as a case in which God was not willing to heal. They would conclude that we can't always be certain that healing is God's will, because if it was God's will, those who had been commissioned to heal the sick would have had no problem in doing so. How quickly we find opportunities to create a theology of excuses! Fortunately, Jesus showed up and healed the boy.

Jesus began by rebuking the disciples as a *"faithless and perverse generation."* I doubt they were expecting such a response. When they asked why they couldn't cast out the demon, Jesus responded, *"Because of your unbelief."* What happened to their faith?

We have created an idea that faith is a static, always-energized power within. We can pray at the drop of a hat because that is what we are supposed to do, but what if we see no results? Were we praying in faith or from routine? It is easy to get confused and begin to look for excuses. This certainly happened to the disciples in this story.

Unbelief is the believer's greatest enemy. It sounds like an oxymoron, but most of us "believers" do learn to live with some level of unbelief in certain areas of our lives. When we discover those areas that are keeping us from fully enjoying the abundant life, we need to go before the Lord and ask Him to purge those areas of unbelief with a revelation of His love and goodness, and then expect Him to do so. Revelation from God is the answer for unbelief.

> Beloved, if our heart does not condemn us, we have confidence toward God. And whatever we ask we receive from Him, because we keep His commandments and do those things that are pleasing in His sight. And this is His commandment: that **we should believe** on the name of His Son Jesus Christ and love one another, as He gave us commandment (1 John 3:21-23).

Unbelief is a response related to our five senses, our logic, how we feel at the moment, whether or not we are in communion with the Lord, and the fact that we often think that what we "know" about faith is faith. Let me say that if the disciples who walked and talked with Jesus for three and a half years and had been commissioned by Him to heal the sick could slide into unbelief, we can too. And yet so many get offended when this possibility is mentioned. The disciples didn't know they were in unbelief and were probably offended that Jesus mentioned it.

Unbelief, knowingly or unknowingly, places more value on the five senses, logic, and the words of others than on God's Word and the finished work of the cross. I am not saying there is malice in our hearts toward the cross or God's promises, but that we simply have not valued those truths to the place that we are unmoved by our senses and the doctor's report.

The faith we live by will be directly related to the relationship we have with the Lord and our sensitivity to His voice. Even the most needy people can have faith leap in their hearts and receive from God. They may not even be born-again believers. It is the believers who seem to have the greater challenge in believing from time to time.

In a perfect scenario, both the afflicted one and the minister will have their faith activated. It only takes one; but when both are seeing the same thing in the Spirit, healing will come. The only thing that can stand in the way of God's will being accomplished is unbelief. This is not just a subject for the sick one, but also for those who pray for the sick. Have we as ministers seen in the Spirit that God has provided for this need? Have we "heard" His Word? Is our faith alive or are we simply ministering from our memories of the past? These are valid questions.

Unbelief is the only force that can stop healing. Unbelief is often undetectable to our senses. Some who outwardly seem very open to healing and proclaim how much faith they have may actually be dealing with unbelief. Sometimes those who appear to be outwardly questioning God and the subject of healing could be in reality very open in their hearts to receive. We can't always know what is going on in someone's heart. Guilt, condemnation, bitterness, unforgiveness, and fear can hinder people from receiving even though they mentally agree with God's provision of healing.

WORD-RELATED FAITH

When Jesus walked the earth healing all who came to Him, the people were in the presence of the physical Jesus whom they could see, hear, and touch. In that sense, their faith was on the level of their five senses. The centurion (Matthew 8:5-12) and the Canaanite woman (Matthew 15:21-28) demonstrated a level of faith that went beyond the sense realm. The centurion said, *"But only speak a word, and my servant will be healed"* (Matthew 8:8). His faith was in the spoken Word, not in a visit to his house by Jesus.

While most of those who went to Jesus were usually healed instantly, and they were being proactive in their faith, it was still a case of being in the presence of a physical Jesus. They were not walking in the same kind of faith that we walk in today. Our faith is not sense-related, but Word-related. Jesus was the Word made flesh to Israel, the revelation of the Word to their five senses. We must approach the written Word—the promises of God and the New Covenant—as they approached Jesus.

...Blessed are they that have not seen, and yet have believed (John 20:29).

If we could get a revelation of the living power of the written Word of God, we would have the same results those who touched Jesus had.

Obviously, people will still have faith in the faith of others and seek healing from someone they can see, hear, and touch. But we are no longer limited in that regard. His Word is living and powerful, and every promise is "yes and amen!" (Hebrews 4:12 and 2 Corinthians 1:20). However, for many this is an area where unbelief can snuff out the power of the Word.

A common thought for many is, *I want a man or woman of God to lay hands on me and I want to feel and see the healing instantly—then I will know I am healed!* This is not the kind of faith we find described in the ministry of Jesus. While the healings we see in the gospel were instant or nearly so, they had already been conceived in the hearts of those who received. They followed Him because they knew they would be healed even before they were healed. We will speak of conceiving healing in a later chapter.

It seems one of the most challenging aspects of our life in Christ is that of having to trust His Word rather than our senses. If we truly believe that His words are Spirit and life (John 6:63), then we must come to the place where we honor His Word over our senses.

> But these are written, that you might believe that Jesus is the Christ, the Son of God; and that believing you might have life through his name (John 20:31).

When we choose to believe what is written, we have life through His name! The flesh profits nothing. Trusting in the flesh profits nothing. Dedicate yourself to believing what is written for you and about you. That is *life!*

True belief springs from true hearing. If you believe that His Word is alive, your heart will be sensitive to hear, and faith will be released. The secret is to believe on His name in every area of our lives, and to love others with His love. We may live in victory in many areas, but still have lingering self-doubt or guilt that has yet to be driven out by the love of God.

> *For this reason I bow my knees to the Father of our Lord Jesus Christ, from whom the whole family in heaven and earth is named, that He would grant you, according to the riches of His glory, to be strengthened with might through His Spirit in the inner man, that Christ may dwell in your hearts through faith; that you, being rooted and grounded in love, may be able to comprehend with all the saints what is the width and length and depth and height—to know the love of Christ which passes knowledge; that you may be filled with all the fullness of God* (Ephesians 3:14-19).

Pray this prayer of Paul, meditate on it, and expect God to flood your heart with a revelation of His love that will drive out unbelief.

Chapter 15

What Can You See?

*And Elisha prayed, and said, "Lord, I pray, open his eyes that he may see." Then **the Lord opened the eyes of the young man, and he saw**. And behold, the mountain was full of horses and chariots of fire all around Elisha* (2 Kings 6:17).

We have spoken of attitudes, expectations and faith, but I want to go a little deeper into the dimension of our spiritual sight or vision. Whether you know it or not, we have two sets of eyes.

Elisha was able to see God's provision with his spiritual eyes, but his servant could not. When the servant's eyes were *"opened,"* he saw what Elisha saw. Just because you are standing next to someone and looking in the same direction doesn't mean that you are seeing what they see. Just because you and the doctor are looking at the same diagnosis doesn't mean you must see the same thing the doctor sees. Spiritual vision is seeing the promises of God accomplished before the natural eyes see the results.

Our natural eyes evaluate the world around us and our possible circumstances in that world. Our natural eyes project us into the future based upon logic, experience, and knowledge. With our natural eyes and natural thinking, we evaluate current circumstances, financial issues, relationship issues, and health issues. We calculate what we see and come to a conclusion about what the future might be like. While all of this is common and natural, it is not spiritual.

Consider the apostle Paul's revelation concerning what we see:

> *While we look not at the things which are seen, but at the things which are not seen. For the things which are seen are temporary, but the things which are not seen are eternal* (2 Corinthians 4:18).

Paul is describing two sets of eyes, those natural and those spiritual. He is saying that the things that are seen with our natural eyes should not determine our focus, but rather what we can see with our spiritual eyes. We are to be focused on eternal things. Temporal things are the things of this life that are subject to change. Everything in this world is subject to change. Relationships are subject to change. Politics are subject to change. Bank accounts are subject to change. Health is subject to change.

Paul exhorts that we should not focus on what is subject to change but rather on what is eternal. How do we see the unseen? How can we escape the trap of only seeing the temporal and living on that level? How can my spiritual sight impact my health and healing?

Now faith is...the evidence of things not seen (Hebrews 11:1).

Once again, we enter into the subject of faith. Faith is not only a response to what we hear—faith comes by hearing the Word of God—but also what we can see with our spiritual eyes. God's words to us should produce a vision. That is how we know we have truly "heard" Him. If there is no vision on the inside, it is doubtful that spiritual hearing has taken place. Our inner vision reflects what we have heard and believed.

"SEE" THE WILL OF GOD

Just a few years ago, my oldest son, David, was hanging Christmas lights on the roof of his in-laws' home. It was a two-story house and David was on a ladder on top of the first roof, working on the lights on the second story roof. The ladder shifted and David fell 20 feet and landed on his head on the sidewalk below. His wife and her family immediately tended to David and began praying for him. My daughter-in-law, Lindsay, called us immediately to tell us what had happened. An ambulance had been called and David seemed incoherent.

As a father, my immediate reaction was to envision the tragic possibilities. Would David live? Would he be para-lyzed? Would he have brain damage. As I was "envisioning" these possibilities, tears were streaming down my face. I then remembered who I was, a child of God, and Who lives within me. I forced myself to "see" a different outcome. I prayed in the Spirit and chose to see David perfectly healed. This was a fight. I would drift back over into my human emotions, and then catch myself and charge back into a vision of victory. This went on for four hours as we received updates from Lindsay.

After four hours, David walked out of the hospital without even a concussion! He was banged up from the fall and had lost some hair, but he was alive and well and has had no side effects since that time.

I am not taking credit for this miracle. Many were agreeing in faith together. But I want to illustrate how necessary it is to "see" the will of God. I could easily have imagined a terrible outcome and unwittingly given authority to that outcome. That seems to be our default, human response. But I chose to see healing and health. It was a fight, but I chose to believe that God's will and God's Word were more powerful than a possible tragedy.

Words create pictures. Unexpected phone calls can create pictures. How we respond and the pictures we choose to see play a huge role in the healing and health that God has for us.

If I speak of a red horse with a green mane and tail, most will attempt to "see" those words. If my wife tells me she wants us to go shopping at a certain store, I will envision the roads that will get us there, the parking lot, and the store. What happens when God declares, *"by My stripes you were healed?"* Can you see it? Many will say no. Why? Because they are using their natural eyes to evaluate their health. All they can see is the doctor's report, the medicine, the symptoms, and a future filled with uncertainty. They are using the eyes of the imagination to project a future of sickness and loss.

Though we often read and hear the Word of God, we just as often fail to "see" ourselves living in those truths. That is the true test as to whether we have actually heard the Word or not. The future we see on the inside is a result of what we have chosen to hear and believe. The health we will harvest is related to the vision of health we carry in our hearts.

> *The lamp of the body is the eye. If therefore your eye is good, your whole body will be full of light. But if your eye is bad, your whole body will be full of darkness…* (Matthew 6:22-23).

I believe we could say that the "life" of the body is also the "light" of the body.

> *In Him was life, and the life was the light of men* (John 1:4).

Life and light are the same thing in this respect. If our spiritual vision is good, in other words, if we see ourselves healed, restored, and enjoying a productive future, we will live from that vision. Our whole body will be full of light. If our spiritual vision is bad, if we are living from our natural eyes and evaluating the future based on the words of others or how we feel, then our futures will conform to what we see. Our bodies will be full of darkness.

YOUR VISION IS YOUR FUTURE

This truth cannot be overstated! Your vision of yourself, your health, and your future, is your faith. It is the evidence of things not yet seen with the natural eyes. What you see on the inside is what is being projected and prepared for consciously or subconsciously. Your vision is your future!

Too often we look at natural problems with our natural eyes and come to natural conclusions. The result is often worry and fear. There is a spiritual dimension to those issues and there are spiritual resources for every need, but the eyes with which you choose to see, and the resulting fear or faith will shape the outcome.

Those who see themselves sick will project their sickness or affliction into the future and make adjustments based upon their natural evaluation. Those who see themselves healed will look past the current challenge and project themselves into a future of health. What is the difference in these two groups? The difference certainly isn't God. The difference is the vision of the heart. The vision of the heart is a harvest of the words we have heard and believed. We are either giving place to words of fear and limitations, or we are giving place to God's promises.

Can you see yourself enjoying a life full of health, joy, and peace? If not, why not? What have you allowed in your heart that projects a different vision? Did you know that Jesus explained that the problems in Israel were due to their hearing, their vision, and their hearts?

> For the hearts of this people have grown dull. Their ears are hard of hearing, and their eyes they have closed, lest they should see with their eyes and hear with their ears, lest they should understand with

their hearts and turn, so that I should heal them (Matthew 13:15).

The multitudes who were sick in Israel were sick because of hardened hearts, closed spiritual eyes, and ears that were not in tune with God.

You are in control of your spiritual eyes. You are in control of what you hear and the pictures it creates. What can you see right now concerning your health? If a vision of a full, healthy life doesn't jump in your heart, then you are listening to the wrong things. Your vision is your future.

HEALING PRAYER

Father, I declare my eyes, ears, and heart to be open to You, Your Word, and Your Spirit. I will hear Your words and I will see what You are doing. I will not allow my heart to be hardened by the circumstances of life. As I become more sensitive to You, healing will flow in my body! Amen!

Chapter 16

The Authority
of the Believer

And when He had called His twelve disciples to Him,
He gave them power over unclean spirits, to cast
them out, and to heal all kinds of sickness and
all kinds of disease (Matthew 10:1).

One of the most powerful revelations we can have in the subject of healing is the revelation of our authority in Christ. What Jesus delegated to His disciples is now inherent in His church.

> *But God, who is rich in mercy, because of His great love with which He loved us, even when we were dead in trespasses, made us alive together with Christ (by grace you have been saved), and raised us up together, and made us sit together in the heavenly places in Christ Jesus* (Ephesians 2:4-6).

As a new creation (2 Corinthians 5:17), seated with Him, filled with His Spirit, and commissioned to take the message of the gospel throughout the world, we carry His authority over the work of the enemy.

Behold, I give you the authority to trample on serpents and scorpions, and over all the power of the enemy, and nothing shall by any means hurt you (Luke 10:19).

Authority over sickness is a function of identity. Authority always flows from the one who knows who he or she is—the boss, the leader, the one in charge. When we see ourselves as God sees us, we will act with His authority. The believer who has a revelation of Christ's authority can use that authority over the works of darkness. God's authority is released through our words, but the words must come from a true understanding of who we are in Christ.

The owner of a business can give instructions to the employees and then leave the office for a few days. The owner doesn't go home and fast and pray and hope that the instructions will be followed. The owner has authority and the employees recognize that authority. His or her identity as the owner establishes beyond a doubt the right to give commands.

As a boy, my father would instruct me to mow the yard while he was away. He fully expected to see a manicured lawn when he returned. I fully expected a session of "correction" if I didn't follow through. I understood my father's authority and my necessary response to that authority.

Born-again Christians have spiritual authority, but most have no idea what that means. Many simply believe that God is in control and He will do what He wants. Few understand that they actually have the authority to be in control over the works of the enemy in their lives.

Until we have a revelation of our identity in Christ, we will remain in the role of a petitioner of God's mercy, but not an enforcer of God's will.

Things know what you believe!

> *So the Lord said, "If you have faith as a mustard seed, you can say to this mulberry tree, 'Be pulled up by the roots and be planted in the sea,' and it would obey you"* (Luke 17:6).

Jesus said that the mulberry tree would obey us! How can a tree obey a person? What is created must submit to a superior authority. No one doubts God's authority to move trees and mountains, but Jesus taught that His authority lives in us!

> *You are of God, little children, and have overcome them, because **He who is in you is greater** than he who is in the world* (1 John 4:4).

Who is in you? Is He greater than sickness? Are you one with Him? Sickness must obey a superior authority. Like a tree or a mountain, sickness can recognize a superior authority. Do you believe that you have authority in the name of Jesus over any sickness or affliction in your body? I am not talking about mental, doctrinal agreement, but a true revelation of your authority in Christ.

> *But he who is joined to the Lord is one spirit with Him* (1 Corinthians 6:17).

While most would say that "God can heal if He wants to," few understand that the authority of Jesus lives in them and that they have the right to walk in that authority.

Authority is a function of identity. Until Christians are convinced of their righteousness and guilt-free standing before God, they will always waver in the area of authority. As long as we see ourselves as victims and put all of the responsibility on God for what happens in our lives, we will never take our true place as sons and daughters and walk in His authority.

> *For if by the one man's [Adam's] offense death reigned through the one, much more those who receive abundance of grace and of the gift of righteousness will reign in life through the One, Jesus Christ* (Romans 5:17).

The abundance of grace and the gift of righteousness have a purpose: that you reign in life! What does it mean to "reign in life?" Should sickness reign over you, or should you, the child of God, reign over sickness?

> *For all the promises of God in Him are Yes, and in Him Amen, to the glory of God through us* (2 Corinthians 1:20).

In the verse from 2 Corinthians 1, the key factor in activating the promises of God is us! We are to reign in life. We are to activate God's promises and enforce His will. Only those who see themselves as God sees them will dare to step into this realm of authority. But it isn't about speaking to a sickness and then waiting to see what happens. That isn't true authority. It is about knowing what will happen before it happens. Faith knows the outcome before it comes out!

FAITH—AUTHORITY IN ACTION

Faith is authority in action! An instruction from God gives you the authority to follow that instruction. A vision from God gives you the authority to move toward and plan for that vision. A quickening from the Holy Spirit about healing is the authority to speak against sickness and declare health and healing.

Faith is not moved by what it sees in the natural world, but by what it sees in the spiritual world of God's provision. When spiritual hearing and seeing take place, the sickness will bow the knee to the higher authority.

A police officer can be identified at a distance as one who has authority. There is a uniform declaring the officer's identity, a badge declaring delegated authority, and a gun revealing potential power. Criminals should recognize police authority and submit to it. If we could only understand that demons and sicknesses are more afraid of Christ's authority in us than many criminals are of the police, we could enter into victorious living as never before.

When my son was declared dead in the womb, the Spirit within me declared "NO!" That was the Spirit of God speaking with authority.

A few years ago I was diagnosed with skin cancer in my ear. A biopsy was done and the doctor informed me that my ear needed surgery for the skin cancer and then plastic surgery to repair the damage. The Spirit within said, "NO." Authority rose up within me. I did not make an appointment as requested. A couple of weeks later a registered letter came in the mail from the doctor declaring the need for surgery followed by plastic surgery. Again, the Spirit within me said "No." Because of that quickening word, I did not follow through with the doctor's instructions.

It took about a year, but my ear slowly healed. It has now been completely healed and free from cancer for a couple of years. My authority in the Lord rose up within me and a divine healing took place!

> *Then He appointed twelve, that they might be with Him and that He might send them out to preach, and to have power to heal sicknesses and to cast out demons* (Mark 3:14-15).

You, too, have been appointed to be with Him. Are you with Him? Are you in communion and fellowship with God on a daily basis? He gave the disciples a purpose to preach and to heal. Do you see your purpose in this life? Your authority will be found in your purpose. Your purpose is to be an overcomer, to be a loving husband or wife, to be a blessing as a father or mother, to be a diligent and faithful employee, etc. You should also have power over sickness in your body and in the bodies of those you love.

Now to Him who is able to do exceedingly abundantly above all that we ask or think, according to the power that works in us (Ephesians 3:20).

The authority of Christ is within you. The Word of God is within you. The Holy Spirit is within you. The promises of God are for you. Sicknesses are not the will of God, but they will stay until a superior authority intervenes. Some sicknesses respond to natural remedies and some to medical remedies, but some will only submit to the authority of Jesus in the heart of the one who knows who they are in Christ.

HEALING PRAYER

Father, I believe You are giving me a deeper revelation of my true identity in You. As I understand the new creation, righteousness, and the Greater One in me, I will become an enforcer of Your will and destroy the works of the enemy in my life, in Jesus' name! Amen!

Chapter 17

Conceiving Healing

How did you become a Christian? How did you receive eternal life? If we can understand this fundamental truth, we should be able to understand a number of Kingdom truths, including healing.

> *Having been born again, not of corruptible seed but incorruptible, through the word of God which lives and abides forever* (1 Peter 1:23).

The idea of being "born again" by the seed of God's Word is language that should produce a picture within; and as they say, a picture is worth a thousand words! When something is born, it is because something was conceived.

Whether we are speaking of the seed of God's Word, or the seed of a man in union with the egg in the woman, we are speaking of life being contained within these "delivery systems." Once the environmental criteria is met—a seed finding soil or a sperm finding an egg—conception takes place. In the case of a seed we would speak of germination, but for the sake of consistency I will use the word conception.

Once something is conceived, there is a divine, preplanned trajectory of growth and eventual birth or fulfillment. The principle put forth in Scripture concerning salvation is known as being "born again." The life of the seed of God's Word found a receptive heart—soil—and conception took place leading to a "new birth." Believers are new creations (2 Corinthians 5:17). Much could be discussed here, but I want to stay within the topic of healing.

Some time back I read the following passage and the Lord spoke to my heart:

> *Let no one say when he is tempted, "I am tempted by God"; for God cannot be tempted by evil, nor does He Himself tempt anyone. But each one is tempted when he is drawn away by his own desires and enticed. Then, when desire has conceived, it gives birth to sin; and sin, when it is full-grown, brings forth death* (James 1:13-15).

This may seem out of place in a book on healing, but I believe there is some revelation here that will be helpful. We will leave to one side the discussion of evil and concentrate on the topic of conception. "*When desire* [cited as *"lust"* in the KJV] *has conceived, it gives birth to sin.*" This is the same principle found in being born again by the incorruptible seed of God's Word. The Word was conceived in your heart and gave birth to a new creation and eternal life with God. In this passage in James, desire or lust is conceived and also gives birth. The baby's name is "sin" and its future is death.

THE BABY'S NAME IS SIN

As I was meditating on this, I felt the Lord speak to me and say, "Barry, if sin and death can be conceived, then health and healing can be conceived." If sickness is simply death in its first stages, then sickness is one of the results of sin's conception. As we have seen, sickness can find a number of opportunities to manifest in our bodies, but its ultimate source was Adam's sin. When Adam and Eve were enticed and gave in to lust, sin was the result and death was the consequence. Sickness was in the package.

Sin was conceived in the Garden of Eden by listening to the words of the enemy. Giving place to words that were not God's words was a fatal mistake. Being receptive to words is an opportunity for conception to take place. We can conceive sin, or we can conceive any number of God's blessings. God's promises are words that carry His nature and authority. We can give heed to the doubt, fear, sarcasm, and unbelief of the world and allow conception in our hearts—or we can choose God's words and allow His life and His promises to be conceived.

> *A good man out of the good treasure of his heart brings forth good things, and an evil man out of the evil treasure brings forth evil things* (Matthew 12:35).

As we read this verse, what is the source of good things or bad things? Is it God's sovereignty as some teach, or is it the human heart? Where is evil desire or lust conceived? In the heart of God, or the human heart? When we understand that the heart can be likened to soil and will seek to "conceive" whatever is planted in it, we can begin to see the means by which God brings healing.

A VISION OF HEALING

Why did the woman with the issue of blood take the risk of being in public—she was "unclean" under the Law of Moses—and press through a crowd in order to touch the hem of Jesus' garment? Why did Blind Bartimaeus cry out louder and louder, so much so that Jesus stopped His journey? Had something been conceived in the hearts of these two suffering people? Why weren't the multitudes of sick people at the Pool of Bethesda (John 5:1-3) seeking Jesus? Why were they content to stay where they were? The knowledge of Jesus and His miracles was everywhere.

For some reason, those at the Pool of Bethesda did not "conceive" a vision of being healed by Jesus. Knowledge about healing is not faith. Faith comes from conception, hearing (Romans 10:17). When something is conceived in the heart, it produces a vision—and a vision produces a declaration!

> *When she heard about Jesus, she came behind Him in the crowd and touched His garment. **For she said**, "If only I may touch His clothes, I shall be made well"* (Mark 5:27-28).

This woman had heard of Jesus, conception, had a vision of touching His clothes, made a declaration about what would happen, and then pursued her vision until it was accomplished. And Jesus was not consciously involved in the healing! Conception led to the birth of her healing!

We can tell what has been conceived in our hearts by the vision we carry within and the declarations that we make. Those who adjust to their physical condition and find ways to live in spite of the affliction, have conceived that adjustment in their hearts. That is the vision they have chosen. Those who carried their friend on a stretcher, climbed onto a roof, opened a hole and lowered their friend through the hole in the presence of Jesus, did so because it was conceived in their hearts. They had a different vision based upon hearing about Jesus.

How do you know if healing has been truly conceived? Conception comes by hearing God's Word in your heart.

So then faith comes by hearing, and hearing by the word of God (Romans 10:17).

Why am I using the word "conception" to speak of faith? Because everything begins with words and springs from words. The words we allow in our hearts are seeds, and they will produce according to the nature of their source. God's words will produce according to their nature and Source—forgiveness, abundant life, peace, joy, love…and healing.

So, how can you know that you are pregnant with healing?

1. Conception will create a new vision for the future. Blind Bartimaeus left his cloak, which identified him as a blind beggar *before* he was healed. He already had a vision of a new identity and left his old identity behind!

*So Jesus stood still and commanded him to be called. Then they called the blind man, saying to him, "Be of good cheer. Rise, He is calling you." **And throwing aside his garment**, he rose and came to Jesus* (Mark 10:49-50).

2. The new vision will create time and perseverance. It's funny how a vision for something we want inspires us to rearrange our priorities and become focused on what has been conceived within. The paralytic man and his four friends would not be denied. Meanwhile, multitudes of sick people were lying around the pool of Bethesda.

Then they came to Him, bringing a paralytic who was carried by four men. And when they could not come near Him because of the crowd, they uncovered the roof where He was. So when they had broken through, they let down the bed on which the paralytic was lying. When Jesus saw their faith, He said to the paralytic, "Son, your sins are forgiven you" (Mark 2:3-5).

3. A vision of healing will bring forth praise and thanksgiving.

Bless the Lord, O my soul; and all that is within me, bless His holy name! Bless the Lord, O my soul, and forget not all His benefits: who forgives all your iniquities, who heals all your diseases, who redeems your life from destruction, who crowns you with lovingkindness and tender mercies, who satisfies your mouth with good things, so that your youth is renewed like the eagle's (Psalm 103:1-5).

Praising God at the time of conception is the evidence of the coming birth. A mother who has become aware of a baby within will spontaneously be thankful and full of praise! In Psalm 103 the benefits that inspire praise are the ongoing forgiveness and healing that is expected. Praise not only remembers the past but anticipates a future of good things!

I cannot tell you how many Christians I have talked to and ministered to over the years who believe mentally in healing and have become offended because they have struggled to experience what they know to be true. I do not want to be insensitive at all, and I understand the genuine desire for and belief in the healing that many are pursuing. But everything in the Kingdom functions according to the concept of seedtime and harvest, or conception as I have described it. A woman can believe in babies, desire a baby, and think she deserves a baby, but until there is conception there will be no baby.

Something existed in the hearts of those who pursued Jesus that was different from those who stayed by the pool of Bethesda. Those at the pool were comfortable in their tradition, culture, and belief system. But there were others who had something conceived in their hearts.

However, the report went around concerning Him all the more; and great multitudes came together to hear, and to be healed by Him of their infirmities (Luke 5:15).

Conception comes from hearing. What is growing in your heart concerning your future health? What is your vision and focus? What are you planning for? What are you talking about? These are clues that will reveal what has actually been conceived within. There is always time to conceive healing. Conception only takes a moment. It can happen right now.

HEALING PRAYER

Father, be it unto me according to Your Word! My heart is open for the supernatural seed of Your Word. Healing is being conceived in my heart right now! Amen!

Chapter 18

How We Are Healed

Because he has set his love upon Me, therefore I
will deliver him; I will set him on high, because he
has known My name. He shall call upon Me, and
I will answer him; I will be with him in trouble; I
will deliver him and honor him. With long life I will
satisfy him, and show him My salvation
(Psalm 91:14-16).

When we speak on the subject of healing, we must begin with the belief that God wants to satisfy us with long life. That is His will. In spite of the corruption of sin and the darkness that is in the world, we should expect long life. Apart from the subject of persecution for our faith, Christians should not die before their time, or before they are satisfied that they have finished their course.

Death through sickness is always a premature death. Death does not require sickness. We are mortal and our bodies will wear out, but sicknesses only speed up death. Death occurs when the spirit leaves the body.

For as the body without the spirit is dead... (James 2:26).

Many precious men and women of God have crossed over into life after death without being sick. This should be our expectation.

Healing, like righteousness, has been imputed to us through the cross. It is available to all. God is not imputing our sins unto us (2 Corinthians 5:19), and He is not making us sick or allowing us to be sick. Sickness, like sin, falls under the dominion of mankind. We choose to sin or not sin, and we can choose to live in health. While there may be challenges, and some challenges are significant, the provision for healing has been made. If we are not convinced of that truth, we will struggle to receive what God has provided.

With our previous discussion of conception in mind, I want to discuss at least seven different ways that healing can be conceived and received. There is no "one size fits all" answer in this subject. Once again, we must be sensitive to the Spirit and follow the faith that is alive in our hearts.

1. Healing by the natural healing process of the body.

God designed the body to heal itself and even in this fallen world with the weaknesses and diseases that sin has unleashed, our bodies still fight to be healthy. This fact alone is a testimony to the truth that God wants us well. If the body is strong enough to heal itself, it will. Healing can occur naturally from many afflictions with or without medical help.

Medical help can be a controversial subject for some. It can't be denied that medical science has done much to save and prolong lives. While an argument can be made that medical action through drugs and other kinds of intervention can produce negative and even dangerous side effects, there are many times that medical help is beneficial and can keep the sick one alive while the body recovers or a healing is conceived.

From time to time we have heard of those who have refused medicine or stopped their medicine in order to prove their faith. Let's be clear that medicine does not stop faith, nor does stopping medicine prove one's faith. Faith does not come or go based upon medicine, but on hearing God's Word. Sadly, some have died because they thought that stopping their medicine was a proof of faith.

Every believer must be led of the Lord and have their faith activated to pursue their health and healing whether it involves medical assistance or not. However, the point remains that many healings occur naturally and over a period of time. Just because a healing is not an instantaneous miracle does not make it any less of a healing. Recovery from sickness is healing.

A number of years ago I suffered an excruciating condition with a kidney stone. At the time I was convinced I was passing multiple stones over a period of months. Each bout with the pain would intensify over the weeks and months until there were times of forty-eight hours or more of total incapacitation. At about the ninth month of suffering, I was in a three-day bout of incredible pain and I finally told my wife that I couldn't take it anymore. I had prayed, declared, believed, and fought the good fight. I was done.

We went to the emergency room where I shuffled in, hunched over like someone who had been shot. I was immediately taken into the emergency area for treatment and after industrial-strength painkillers and an MRI, I was told I had one enormous kidney stone that had been in the process of being expelled for the last nine months. The doctor declared that there was no way this stone would pass on its own and that I needed medical intervention.

When the doctor explained the intervention to me, faith was conceived! All I needed to hear was what he proposed to do and I knew I had *no faith* for that! My spirit was stirred to believe God. I went home in faith and two days later the giant stone passed with no pain!

During the previous months of intermittent pain and agony, I had thought I was in faith. I was "doing" what I knew to do. I was frustrated like anyone would be. But for some reason, faith leapt in my heart when I heard the negative word of the doctor! Because there is a deep foundation of the Word in my life, a contrary word was all it took to stir my faith.

Could I have accepted the doctor's words? Yes, and there would have been no condemnation from God. In 1987, I was diagnosed with a malignant melanoma on my back. In this case I had it removed along with about 4 inches of skin around the area of the melanoma. I had faith and peace to receive medical assistance. We must all come to a place of faith, and faith comes from hearing God.

2. Healing by the Word.

The very nature of God's Word is life and health.

> *My son, give attention to my words; incline your ear to my sayings. Do not let them depart from your eyes; keep them in the midst of your heart; for they are life to those who find them, and health to all their flesh* (Proverbs 4:20-22).

When we spend quality time in the Word, allowing God to reveal His truth to us, it is health to our flesh. Healing is conceived by the Word of God. We don't even need to be studying the subject of healing. The very nature of God's Word is life and health.

While many would follow a doctor's instructions to take a certain medicine four times a day for two or three weeks, they won't take seriously what God said about the power of His Word! His Word is health—remedy, cure—to our flesh.

> *The words that I speak unto you, they are spirit, and they are life* (John 6:63).

The most inspiring New Testament writings on the subject of healing are the four gospels. Reading the stories of healing in the gospels over and over again will help create the expectation in your own heart for healing and health. His Word is alive and active!

> *For the word of God is living and powerful, and sharper than any two-edged sword...* (Hebrews 4:12).

Believe that the same Spirit that raised Christ from the dead shall also quicken your mortal body!

> *But if the Spirit of Him who raised Jesus from the dead dwells in you, He who raised Christ from the dead will also give life to your mortal bodies through His Spirit who dwells in you* (Romans 8:11).

While this can certainly refer to the resurrection when Jesus returns, it is not limited to that context. Consider another of Paul's statements about the mortal body.

> *Therefore do not let sin reign in your mortal body, that you should obey it in its lusts* (Romans 6:12).

Paul is not referring to our dead bodies in this statement, but rather to our earthly bodies while alive. God will give life to our mortal bodies through His Spirit who dwells in us! Believing is receiving. Let the Word conceive healing in your body.

3. Miracle healing.

We all love the subject of miracles! A miracle is often seen as a divine intervention that transcends any human participation. But is that entirely accurate?

Miracles are not limited to the ministry of healing. Miracles in the Bible include the multiplication of the loaves and fishes, stilling storms, walking on water, and raising the dead. When speaking of healing, we often think of a miracle as an instantaneous healing.

Some think of a miracle as simply a whim of God. He arbitrarily decides to get involved and heal someone instantly. Such a view has led to much confusion, doubt, and heartache for many Christians. Some might ask, "If God can do miracles and He hasn't done one for me, does He really love me at all?" "Have I done something to deserve this sickness?"

When we look more closely at the subject of miracles, we can see that there are spiritual laws in place that can be activated according to God's Word, not according to divine whims.

> *Therefore He who supplies the Spirit to you and works miracles among you, does He do it by the works of the law, or by the hearing of faith?* (Galatians 3:5)

How do miracles happen? They are a result of the *hearing of faith*. In other words, miracles are faith-related, not haphazard and unpredictable. The miracles of Jesus were because He had heard the Father and responded to what He heard and saw.

> *Then Jesus answered and said to them, "Most assuredly, I say to you, the Son can do nothing of Himself, but what He sees the Father do; for whatever He does, the Son also does in like manner"* (John 5:19).

Nothing that Jesus did was based upon a whim of the moment. In His time of prayer with the Father, He saw the healings, the storms stilled, and the multitudes fed. He did nothing of Himself. This is the key. It isn't that God is picking and choosing when to release His power, it is whether or not we have spent time with Him to "see" such things with our spiritual eyes. Perhaps we are often expecting results before "seeing" what the Father is doing. Not even Jesus did that.

Signs and wonders follow the preaching of the Word. When a preacher of the Word and the listeners are expecting God's power to be released, it will be!

> *And they went out and preached everywhere, the Lord working with them and confirming the word through the accompanying signs. Amen* (Mark 16:20).

When people hear the gospel of the Kingdom, receptive hearts respond. The *"hearing of faith,"* conception, takes place (Galatians 3:5). Proactive and reactive faith are stirred up and miracles happen! Before I knew my wife, and while she was an unbeliever, she attended a meeting where she heard the message of healing. Faith came and she was healed instantly of a back issue. Later in the same service, she was born again! Healing and forgiveness are the same gospel message.

Miracles follow the declaration of the name of Jesus! In Acts chapter 3, Peter and John encountered a lame man on the steps of the temple. Peter "saw" something in the Spirit and acted accordingly. He declared the name of Jesus and grabbed the hand of the crippled man.

> *"...In the name of Jesus Christ of Nazareth, rise up and walk." And he took him by the right hand and lifted him up, and immediately his feet and ankle bones received strength. So he, leaping up, stood*

and walked and entered the temple with them—
walking, leaping, and praising God (Acts 3:6-8).

I don't believe you can lift someone who has no intention of being lifted by just grabbing a person's hand. Something in the declaration that Peter made impacted the lame man to respond. Even that simple declaration of Peter's faith created reactive faith in the cripple and a miracle occurred!

Throughout the gospels and the book of Acts we find miracles happening—and in every case they can be traced to someone's response to God's Word. Healing meetings are wonderful opportunities to hear and be healed! (See Luke 5:15.)

4. Healing by a gift of healing.

A gift of healing is simply a healing miracle or obvious recovery that can be attributed to faith in God's Word. Gifts of healing may not always be instantaneous but in the world of the unseen, the healing has begun and the body is responding. The healing is conceived in the heart by the hearing of faith that releases the power of God. Either the one ministering has seen and heard God, or the one receiving has seen and heard God.

The woman with the issue of blood knew she would be healed if she only touched the hem of Jesus' robe. Jesus was not actively participating in this miracle gift of healing. His faith was not involved. But He is always yes and amen (2 Corinthians 1:20) and her faith took the gift that is offered to all.

5. Healing through the faith of the family or those with authority in the life of the sick one.

Healing is not limited to the faith of the afflicted one or the faith of a minister. Loved ones or those who care for sick ones can also conceive healing and release faith for their healing. We have at least two examples in the gospels.

> *Now when Jesus had entered Capernaum, a centurion came to Him, pleading with Him, saying, "Lord, my servant is lying at home paralyzed, dreadfully tormented"* (Matthew 8:5-6).

A Roman centurion who had no covenant with God and was not included in the promises of God for Israel, nevertheless had faith to approach Jesus on behalf of his servant. His relationship to his servant is mentioned in Luke.

> *And a certain centurion's servant, who was dear to him, was sick and ready to die* (Luke 7:2).

It could be said that the motivation of the centurion was love. While the servant was not a blood relative, the love of the centurion was the motivation for his faith. Jesus responded with grace and the servant was healed.

> *And behold, a woman of Canaan came from that region and cried out to Him, saying, "Have mercy on me, O Lord, Son of David! My daughter is severely demon-possessed"* (Matthew 15:22).

In this story, there is a Gentile woman, not of the covenant, appealing to Jesus on behalf of her daughter. The motivation again was love. Without going into the whole story, the faith that sprang from love was answered by the grace of God. Her daughter was healed.

The point is that the faith of loved ones can bring healing to those who are too afflicted to hear the Word or release their own faith. There is grace in love.

And the grace of our Lord was exceedingly abundant, with faith and love which are in Christ Jesus (1 Timothy 1:14).

6. Healing through the prayer of agreement.

Years ago, while pastoring a church in Chile, a visitor came to me after the service and asked for prayer. She explained that she had been diagnosed with bone cancer and she was obviously distraught. At that moment I didn't have a conviction that either one of us was in faith for her healing. She was from a Catholic background and had heard of our church and the healings that were taking place, but she was coming to me in more of an emotional state than a state of faith.

I asked her if she would be willing to read a book on healing first, and then return for prayer the following week. I gave her a book by T.L. Osborn in Spanish and sent her home. A week later she returned for prayer, and I could see a difference in her face. I asked if she had read the book and she had, and she now knew that God wanted her well. Healing had been conceived in her! We agreed together in prayer.

Perhaps a month later she returned and told me that her latest medical examinations had revealed no cancer at all; and on top of that, her vision had been healed and had returned to 20/20! Agreement is a powerful thing, especially when it begins with agreement with God and His Word.

Again I say to you that if two of you agree on earth concerning anything that they ask, it will be done for them by My Father in heaven. For where two or three are gathered together in My name, I am there in the midst of them (Matthew 18:19-20).

While this passage is found in the context of church discipline, the wording allows us to see a concept that transcends the particular context. Agreeing as concerning *"anything"* brings us to a place of understanding the incredible power of agreement. When we apply this concept to the subject of healing, we have discovered a tremendous channel of healing.

We are only in true biblical agreement when our hearts have agreed with God's Word and we have been quickened in our faith. Those who truly agree have seen the same answer and heard the same word from God. Healing has been conceived in their hearts. If one person can put a thousand to flight, then what is the power of two or more in agreement?

James touches on this subject in a little different context.

Is anyone among you sick? Let him call for the elders of the church, and let them pray over him, anointing him with oil in the name of the Lord. And the prayer of faith will save the sick, and the Lord will raise him up. And if he has committed

*sins, he will be forgiven. Confess your trespasses
to one another, and pray for one another, that you
may be healed. The effective, fervent prayer of a
righteous man avails much* (James 5:14-16).

There is much revelation in this passage. The first thing
we notice is that James considers sickness in the church to
be unacceptable. *"Is anyone among you sick?"* The question
implies that there shouldn't be anyone sick in the church.
Unfortunately, in many of our modern churches the question
could be, "Is there anyone here who is not sick?" So many
Christians are suffering, and the church often does not have
an answer.

The next thing we notice is that the elders of the church
should be able to pray the prayer of faith. Again, in today's
modern church there may be elders who do not have faith.
They have been taught that healing passed away, or God uses
sickness to perfect us, or He will only heal if it is His will.
Such double-mindedness makes faith impossible. The prayer
of faith can only be prayed if there is no doubt about God's
will and His provision.

We read on to find that the prayer of faith will *"raise up"*
the afflicted one. From this we can understand that not all
healing is instantaneous, but the prayer of faith will activate
the healing process. We also find the subject of sin and how
personal sin can be the reason for the sickness. This has been
discussed earlier in this book.

We then come to verse 16 of James 5. *"Pray for one another
that you may be healed."* This would fall into the category of
the prayer of agreement. Notice in James 5 that sins are being

confessed to one another before the prayer of agreement is prayed. Once again, unforgiveness, bitterness, and strife should be dealt with if we are going to be in a place of confident expectation and agreement. There is still grace for every situation, but if we are aware of anything that could hinder our hearts from believing, we should deal with that.

When Christians agree, it is because they have seen the unseen and heard from God. Such unity in the area of healing will produce an *"effective, fervent prayer"* (James 5:16).

If you are afflicted, find someone who shares your faith, someone who is willing to spend time with God to see the answer and agree with God's provision for your need. Don't ask those to pray who will only agree that you are sick. Find those who agree that by His stripes you were healed!

7. Healing through the faith of the sick person.

We have already covered the topic of faith and from where it comes. I am listing the various channels of healing that are available and have hopefully given a good explanation of personal faith in an earlier chapter.

HEALING PRAYER

Father, I will be sensitive to Your Spirit and Your leading and expect healing to be conceived in my heart and received through any possible channel. Amen!

Chapter 19

Health Is a Harvest

One of the most important revelations we must have for successful Christian living is the revelation of sowing and reaping. Jesus declared that the Kingdom of God functions according to this spiritual law.

> *And He said, "The kingdom of God is as if a man should scatter seed on the ground, and should sleep by night and rise by day, and the seed should sprout and grow, he himself does not know how. For the earth yields crops by itself: first the blade, then the head, after that the full grain in the head. But when the grain ripens, immediately he puts in the sickle, because the harvest has come"* (Mark 4:26-29).

This parable, when fully understood, can transform our lives on every level. Everything in life is responding to the principle of seedtime and harvest. This is how God created the earth. Every seed is created to reproduce according to its kind, and in every seed there exists the potential for infinite harvests.

Redemption is a function of sowing and reaping. Jesus was the Seed who had to fall into the earth and die that He might bring forth much fruit—you and me!

> *Most assuredly, I say to you, unless a grain of wheat falls into the ground and dies, it remains alone; but if it dies, it produces much grain* (John 12:24).

God's desire was to harvest many sons and daughters who bear His image. God's method to receive what He wanted was to sow His Son into the earth. The new creation requires new births. Jesus was the firstborn from the dead in this new creation. When we got born again, we became part of that new creation.

> *For whom He foreknew, He also predestined to be conformed to the image of His Son, that He might be the firstborn among many brethren* (Romans 8:29).

We are born again through the same spiritual law of seed-time and harvest:

> *Having been born again, not of corruptible seed but incorruptible, through the word of God which lives and abides forever* (1 Peter 1:23).

As we read the Scriptures, we can find this principle throughout. Our eternal life and born-again spirit is a harvest. Our renewed mind is a harvest. The fruit of the Spirit is a harvest—and in every fruit, there is a seed!

What about physical health? Undoubtedly our health is also a harvest. What we sow into our lives in all three dimensions—spirit, soul, and body—will follow the principle of seedtime and harvest. Seeds produce after their kind, and the harvest is always greater than the seed from which it was conceived.

> *Beloved, I pray that you may prosper in all things and*
> *be in health, just as your soul prospers* (3 John 2).

In this verse, John is linking health and prosperity to the condition and prosperity of the soul. In other words, the prosperity of the soul will impact the harvest in the area of health.

When we realize that everything around us is potential seed, and we understand that every seed we allow into our lives carries a potential harvest, then we can begin to understand how to adjust our lives in order to have the greatest possible harvest of health.

What we feed on is the fuel of our lives. Our bodies feed on food, our minds feed on information, our souls feed on events, relationships, and emotions, and our spirits must feed on the Word, which is Spirit.

> *Your words were found, and I ate them, and Your*
> *word was to me the joy and rejoicing of my heart...*
> (Jeremiah 15:16).

Which kind of "food" is more important to you? The answer will reveal a lot about your present and your future health on every level. Those who focus on natural food will talk about food, think about food, crave food, and live their lives around food. Even health food can become a distraction if we aren't living by every word that proceeds from the mouth of God. Humans cannot live on bread alone. Not even whole wheat, organic bread.

Those who feed on information will fill their minds with all the latest news on whatever subject that interests them. They struggle when separated from the latest news. It is what satisfies them.

Those who live only from the soul, struggle if they aren't continually happy emotionally and in their relationships.

While all of these areas comprise the reality of our lives, they should not be the source of our lives. We are spiritual beings created to live by and feed on the Word of God. Jesus said, *"Man shall not live on bread alone but by every word that proceeds from the mouth of God"* (Matthew 4:4). In other words, though we must eat and relate to our world and those around us, those areas cannot be the source of our lives. Only His words can satisfy and give us the strength and wisdom to live above the corruption in the world.

If your focus and passion isn't God's Word, you will never be satisfied. The other areas I've mentioned will begin to dominate your life and leave you unfulfilled and stressed. A spirit that is nourished on God's words will produce life and peace.

> *I am the vine, you are the branches. He who abides in Me, and I in him, bears much fruit; for without Me you can do nothing* (John 15:5).

Abiding in Him is a form of sowing His life into ours. Health is more than physical. As noted earlier, every part of our being is connected to the other parts. Our mental health, emotional health, spiritual health, and physical health all impact each other. If we are going to harvest physical health, we must sow into all areas of our lives with the proper seed.

Sowing bitterness and stress can impact our health. Sowing fear, or allowing fear to be sown into us, can eventually weaken our health. Sowing poor food choices can eventually harvest health issues that will in turn create mental and emotional hardships.

GOD'S WORD—OUR MAIN SOURCE

Health is a harvest! The more we understand how God designed creation and the spiritual laws that govern all things, the more we can actively participate in our own health and prosperity.

God's Word should be our main source of seed.

> *For as the rain comes down, and the snow from heaven, and do not return there, but water the earth, and make it bring forth and bud, that it may give seed to the sower and bread to the eater, so shall My word be that goes forth from My mouth; it shall not return to Me void, but it shall accomplish what I please, and it shall prosper in the thing for which I sent it* (Isaiah 55:10-11).

God's Word will reproduce according to its kind. It will accomplish its purpose if it finds good soil. Our hearts are the soil that the Word of God needs. As we sow God's promises and wisdom into our hearts, our bodies will conform to

Truth. Spiritual revelations of God's goodness and love will set us free from fear, worry, stress, and bad choices. The harvest of spiritual health will impact our emotional and mental health. As the soul prospers, our physical health will improve as well (3 John 2).

We will harvest what we cooperate with. A farmer will harvest from the seed he has sown, watered, and cultivated. If he allows weeds into his field and does nothing, he is cooperating with weeds and the harvest will reflect it. We are either cooperating with God's design and purpose, or we are cooperating with a fallen world, the flesh and the devil. Our health on every level is at stake.

Many Christians fail to realize that just because they believe in healing doesn't mean they will reap healing. Just because you believe in watermelons doesn't mean you will reap watermelons. Watermelon seeds must be planted and cultivated if you plan to eat watermelon. Your mental agreement with watermelons doesn't grow them. They must be sown and harvested.

So it is with health. Our lives are harvests of past seed sown. Let me hasten to add that in spite of the harvests you may be reaping right now, there is grace for healing and miracles in your life. God has made provision for you. That is the good news! But to neglect the subject of why we might be suffering would be negligent. If we don't learn to cooperate with Kingdom truth, we can get sick again and again.

*My son, give attention to my words; incline your
ear to my sayings. Do not let them depart from
your eyes; keep them in the midst of your heart; for*

they are life to those who find them, and health to all their flesh (Proverbs 4:20-22).

Sowing God's Word into our lives continually will be health to our flesh, our bodies. There is a physical impact from the Spirit of the Word! Jesus said the same:

…The words that I speak to you are spirit, and they are life (John 6:63).

The more we sow God's Word into our lives, the more our health will improve on every level. Mental health, emotional health, and physical health will all be impacted by the incorruptible seed of God's Word. The secret to a healthy life isn't only the kind of food you eat, but the Word that you hear. Health is a harvest!

Declare the following:

> *By His stripes I am healed! His Word is life and health to my flesh. His Spirit quickens my mortal body. Life and health is in the power of my tongue. The fruit of my righteousness is a tree of life. He sent His Word and healed me!*
>
> *I bless the Lord with all that is within me. I bless the Lord and forget none of His benefits. He has forgiven all my iniquities and healed all my diseases. He has redeemed my life from destruction and crowned me with lovingkindness and tender mercy. He satisfies my mouth with good things so that my youth is renewed like the eagles!*

Chapter 20

The Struggle to Understand

Why does a young parent suffer and die from cancer? Why are children born with afflictions that end their lives early? Why do many Christians seem to suffer the same diseases as non-Christians?

Questions like these are asked by believers around the world as they struggle with the tragedy of the death of loved ones long before their time. Sadly, in many churches these believers are instructed to trust in the sovereignty of God and accept the fact that He was in control of these events.

Could this possibly be true? In many of these same churches the doctrine of healing is not taught and sometimes even attacked as false. Even while precious saints are suffering and dying in their churches, they offer no answers and disparage those who believe that it is God's will to heal.

God is not participating in the untimely deaths of anyone, nor does He determine who is saved and who is lost. God has given us the gospel of His power (Romans 1:17) that brings salvation, both spiritual and physical, to all who believe. The choice is ours. Power and authority over sickness has been invested in the church. We must quit wallowing in unbelief and preach the Truth so that the multitudes may be saved and healed.

> *...great multitudes came together to hear, and to be healed by Him of their infirmities* (Luke 5:15).

Jesus is the same yesterday, today, and forever (Hebrews 13:8). If the multitudes in Israel could come to hear Him and be healed, the same opportunity is available to us. Jesus did not classify some as worthy of healing and others as unworthy. He did not point out personal sin and refuse to heal. He did not explain that the sickness was to teach or perfect the afflicted one. Jesus shared the Word and all who heard and believed were healed.

Jesus has set the church against sickness. You are a vessel of healing for others. The Healer and His healing power reside in you. You are not the sick, trying to get well. You are the healed, resisting sickness. You must see yourself as healed, as victorious, as more than a conqueror and as able to do all things through Christ who strengthens you!

Those who receive from God see themselves receiving from God before the manifestation. They are convinced that Jesus has made them worthy and they put themselves in a position to receive what they see as their right. The multitudes wouldn't have followed after Jesus if they believed He would condemn them and refuse to heal them. There was grace for all who came. They could see the end of their affliction in the presence of Jesus.

We must see ourselves as God sees us. Faith is not a mental exercise but a spiritual revelation of Jesus in us. His healing and authority are in us. We can speak to sickness as we would speak to our disobedient dog. The dog must obey. We have no doubt. There are times when we must attack the problem as if it were a snake in the house. What would you do with a snake in your house? Some fearful people might leave home and never come back. Others might learn to live in the house in fear, knowing that the snake may strike them at any moment. But some would say, "No way am I going to live like this." And they would find the snake and kill it.

When you are sure of who you are in Christ and who Christ is in you, and when you see how the enemy has treated you and stolen your health, and when you realize that the God of the universe lives in you, healing will be conceived. You will rise up in faith and authority and speak to your body and command that it submit to the Word of God.

> *For all the promises of God in Him are Yes, and in Him Amen, to the glory of God through us* (2 Corinthians 1:20).

The disciples were granted authority over all sickness. Their authority was delegated during Jesus' time on earth. Our authority is inherent! The Greater One lives in us! There is no greater authority.

> *And when He had called His twelve disciples to Him, He gave them power over unclean spirits, to cast them out, and to heal all kinds of sickness and all kinds of disease* (Matthew 10:1).

Heal the sick, cleanse the lepers, raise the dead, cast out devils. Freely you have received, freely give (Matthew 10:8).

He sent them to preach the kingdom of God and to heal the sick (Luke 9:2).

And heal the sick that are there, and say to them, "The kingdom of God is come near to you" (Luke 10:9).

[Believers] *will lay hands on the sick, and they will recover* (Mark 16:18).

Not only is His authority in you for you to be healed, it is in you to bring healing to others. Do you believe this?

Even if you are suffering as you read this, a revelation of God's healing power in you for others can bring healing to your own life. As we give, we receive. You have been given His authority over sickness!

What about the man born blind?

Now as Jesus passed by, He saw a man who was blind from birth. And His disciples asked Him, saying, "Rabbi, who sinned, this man or his parents, that he was born blind?" Jesus answered, "Neither this man nor his parents sinned, but that the works of God should be revealed in him. I must work the works of Him who sent Me while it is day; the night is coming when no one can work. As long as I am

*in the world, I am the light of the world." When He
had said these things, He spat on the ground and
made clay with the saliva; and He anointed the
eyes of the blind man with the clay. And He said
to him, "Go, wash in the pool of Siloam" (which
is translated, Sent). So he went and washed, and
came back seeing* (John 9:1-7).

Many are confused by this story and some believe that
God made this man blind for a divine purpose. The conclusion is that sometimes God puts sickness on people for His
glory. There are many problems with this interpretation.

First of all, nobody was giving God glory while the man was
blind. No one was giving God glory for the multitudes of sick
people in Israel. If sickness is for God's glory, then Jesus was
working against the will of God by healing all who came to Him.

Sickness is a product of sin in the earth. Sin has corrupted
even the genetics of mankind. Again, I am not referring necessarily to personal sin, but simply the destructive power of
sin in humanity. Jesus points out in this story that neither this
man nor his parents were responsible for the man's blindness. Humanity is suffering from the law of sin and death.
However, every sickness is an opportunity for the works of
God! In other words, His work is healing, not sickness. God
gets glory from restoring lives, not from leaving them in distress. If sickness is for God's glory, then healing should never
be expected or sought.

Jesus healed all who came to Him for the glory of God.
Healing is just as much God's heart today as it was in Jesus'
day. Healing glorifies God!

HEALING PRAYER

Father, I will declare that it is Your nature and heart to heal. I have no doubt. Healing brings You glory and I will live for Your glory! Amen!

Chapter 21

Jesus' Purpose

Everything that God has created has a purpose. Though sin in the earth perverted the purpose of much of God's creation, the idea of purpose remains intact. The purpose of mankind was to be fruitful and multiply and have dominion in the earth (Genesis 1:26-28). The purpose of seeds is to reproduce abundantly according to their kind. One of the purposes of God's Word is to be health to our flesh.

When we don't understand the purpose of something, we will abuse it or lose its potential benefit. If I don't understand the purpose of a flat-screen TV, I may use it for a snow sled. Ignorance of God's purposes in creation has unleashed suffering and misery around the world.

Yet, "*we know that all things work together for good to those who love God, to those who are the called **according to His purpose***" (Romans 8:28).

When we walk in God's purpose for our lives, God causes circumstances to work together for our good, even when we make mistakes. However, if we are walking according to our own lusts and desires, we should not expect the same results.

Satan, in his rebellion and desire to resist God's purpose, has a purpose to *"steal, kill, and destroy"* (John 10:10). The darkness that sin has brought to the world, coupled with the spiritual force of wickedness at work in the hearts of many, allows corruption, loss, suffering, sickness, and death to reach into many of our lives.

THE POWER OF PURPOSE

For this reason Jesus came with a purpose, or we could say with many purposes. Jesus came to seek and save what was lost. Jesus came that we might have abundant life. Jesus came to fulfill the Law and give His life as a ransom for many. The list could go on and on.

> *…For this purpose the Son of God was manifested, that He might destroy the works of the devil* (1 John 3:8).

First John 3:8 describes one of Jesus' primary purposes—to destroy the works of the devil.

Let's consider the power of purpose for a moment. A hunting dog has been bred with a purpose. A guard dog has been bred and trained for a purpose. A seeing-eye dog has been trained for a purpose. A sheep dog is bred for a purpose. Those dogs are most fulfilled and excited when they are accomplishing their purpose. Dogs that are never released into their purpose will never experience the joy of that purpose or destiny.

Jesus came with a purpose—to destroy the works of the devil. In other words, Jesus is excited and fulfilled when His presence is bringing destruction to the world of darkness and suffering.

First John 3:8 reveals a number of important facts:

1. There is a devil.

2. The devil has works.

3. The devil's works are worthy of destruction.

4. Jesus came to destroy the devil's works.

When we meditate on this verse we must come to the conclusion that not all that happens in the world is God's will. There are things that happen in our lives that are not of God but rather the work of the enemy. Anything that brings loss, suffering, destruction, sickness, and death is not God's will! In fact, those are the things that Jesus came to destroy! It is His purpose!

> *...God anointed Jesus of Nazareth with the Holy Spirit and with power, who went about doing good and healing all who were oppressed by the devil, for God was with Him* (Acts 10:38).

Sickness is a work of the devil. Regardless of how the sickness came to be and whether or not it has natural or spiritual roots, it still reflects the corruption of Adam's sin and darkness, not the abundant life of God. This is so incredibly important to understand. The moment we give place to the idea that a sickness is from God, we have lost the battle. There can be no faith. There can be no authority.

Jesus healed all who were oppressed of the devil because it was His purpose! God was with Him, and in the presence of God there can be no corruption or sickness. All who came to Jesus were healed because healing was His purpose. The work of the enemy, regardless of the root that brought sickness, was worthy of destruction. That is grace!

When we are able to see sickness as a work of the enemy and a fruit of Adam's sin, and see Jesus with a purpose to destroy it, something rises up on the inside and we begin to get the right attitude and have the right expectation. Authority comes to life and like killing a snake in the house, we begin to cooperate with God's will for our lives.

Sadly, many have a different view of God. In their understanding His purpose is to test us with sickness and to allow hardships in our lives for His mysterious will. When we have a wrong view of God, we will be candidates for the works of the enemy and we will never allow Jesus to do what He came to do. He came to destroy the works of the devil in your life.

HEALING PRAYER

Father, I will walk in Your purpose to destroy the works of the enemy! You came to heal the sick and set the captives free, and I will not be a victim of the enemy! Amen!

Chapter 22

Who Is Lord?

Speaking in a general sense, our Lord is to whom we continually and faithfully submit. We may say that Jesus is our Lord, but if we are faithfully submitting to other things, the other things are really our lord.

> *Do you not know that to whom you present yourselves slaves to obey, you are that one's slaves whom you obey...* (Romans 6:16).

Let's return to the example of a man who was a slave to his circumstances. In John chapter 5, we have the story of the man who had been lying by the Pool of Bethesda for thirty-eight years due to a physical affliction. We have discussed this multitude earlier. This man was waiting for a supposed stirring of the waters by an angel, at which time the first one into the water would be healed.

In this brief description, we can find this man submitted to two different "lords" that dominated his life. First, he was a slave to his affliction. It had dictated his lifestyle for thirty-eight long years. His identity, routine, and destiny revolved around the sickness. The sickness had become his lord.

Second, he was being lorded over by a superstition, in my opinion. His belief held him captive to a pool of water. There is no mention in the Old Testament of healing coming to Israel by means of an angel stirring the waters of a pool. Yet, a multitude of people had submitted to this story.

> *When Jesus saw him lying there, and knew that he already had been in that condition a long time, He said to him, "Do you want to be made well?"* (John 5:6)

Jesus presented this man with a new option. The new option would mean that the lordships of sickness and superstition would have to release their grip, and the man would be able to enter in to true freedom if he was willing to release his grip on those two masters!

Whatever truly rules over our lives, determines our destinies, limits our options, and must be consulted for all of life's decisions, is our true lord. It may be the lordship of fear, of lack, of guilt, or of sickness. When we approach the topic of healing from this perspective, it puts a new light on the subject.

Saying that Jesus is Lord and actually living under His lordship are two different things. The Lord Jesus Christ has no sickness in the Kingdom He has given us. He has given us all things that pertain to life and godliness (2 Peter 1:4). He is able to do exceedingly, abundantly more than we ask or think according to the power that works in us! (See Ephesians 3:20.)

Establishing Jesus as Lord is an act of your will and a decision to reject anything that doesn't reflect the heart and will of God. If the thief, Satan, comes to steal, kill, and destroy (John 10:10), then that is not the Kingdom of the Lord Jesus. His Kingdom is abundant life, not chronic sickness.

Changing lords may take some time. Our minds must be renewed and our hearts fully persuaded that Jesus is Lord.

> *And do not be conformed to this world, but be transformed by the renewing of your mind, that you may prove what is that good and acceptable and perfect will of God* (Romans 12:2).

> [Abraham] *being fully convinced that what He [God] had promised He was also able to perform* (Romans 4:21).

Many times we allow circumstances, superstitions, fear, and wrong thinking to be our lords without even realizing it. We claim that Jesus is Lord, but we live in bondage to other lords. True freedom, including healing, can come when we choose to make Jesus our true Lord.

Do you want to be free? Do you want to be made well? Submit yourself—your heart, mind, and destiny—to the lordship of Jesus. Let go of the lordship of circumstances. True freedom can begin with the recognition of the lordship of bondage and the decision to fire that master and give your heart to the One who loves you and wants to set you free.

> *Therefore if the Son makes you free, you shall be free indeed* (John 8:36).

ANY REASON WHY NOT?

Is there any reason that you can't be healed? The question is meant to probe the depths of your heart. If you can come up with *any* reason to explain why you can't be healed, then we've discovered why you aren't healed. That reason represents double-mindedness.

> *But let him ask in faith, with no doubting, for he who doubts is like a wave of the sea driven and tossed by the wind. For let not that man suppose that he will receive anything from the Lord; he is a double-minded man, unstable in all his ways* (James 1:6-8).

Doubt must be replaced with the Truth. You must believe that there is *no* reason why you can't be healed. There is no other Lord but Jesus!

Are you worthy to be healed? If the question causes you to pause and reflect, then we've discovered why you aren't healed. Jesus has taken our sicknesses and our sins on the cross. It has nothing to do with your worthiness. He is worthy and He has given forgiveness and healing to all.

If healing is available to anyone, it is available to everyone—just like forgiveness of sin. Jesus healed all who came to Him, and He never held a pre-healing interview to determine if the sick person was worthy or not. By His stripes we *were* healed (1 Peter 2:24).

Is God willing to heal you? Answering with a yes or no isn't really the way to go with this question. The fact is, God has already provided healing for every person on earth. It isn't a matter of His will. It is a matter of receiving what has been provided. His will has been forever revealed through Jesus.

Jesus dealt with the root of sickness on the cross. It is called sin. If the root has been dealt with, the fruit, sickness, has also been dealt with. In the same way that salvation is available to all people, healing is available to all.

Just as we receive the gift of salvation by faith, we can receive healing. It's not about who you are or what you have done, it is about what He did that you can receive freely. Healing is for you. If you believe it, you can receive it.

The Truth of the gospel must be your Lord if you are going to walk in health.

HEALING PRAYER

Father, I declare Jesus the Lord of my life! I will break the bondage of other lords and submit fully to the lordship of Jesus. I will not be bound to sickness and lorded over by physical affliction. The Son has set me free! Amen!

Chapter 23

What About Paul's Thorn?

Many struggle with biblical stories that bring doubt to their hearts. While I have dealt with a number of stories thus far, I will take some time to consider other moments in Scripture that are often used to steal faith.

One of the most often used New Testament passages to suggest that God uses sickness is found in 2 Corinthians 12, concerning Paul's thorn in the flesh.

> *And lest I should be exalted above measure by the abundance of the revelations, a thorn in the flesh was given to me... (2 Corinthians 12:7).*

Many traditional interpretations of this verse conclude that God made Paul sick due to the abundance of revelations that He gave him. Despite the glaring inconsistency in that reasoning, this passage has been used to steal the faith of multitudes. Many will say, "If Paul's sickness was from God, maybe mine is as well." Instantly, the revelation of the cross, of redemption, of Jesus' ministry, the healing gifts given to the church, the miracles in the book of Acts, and the revelation of God's nature throughout the Bible are discarded, and Paul's thorn is exalted as "Exhibit A" in the case against divine healing.

Let us break down Paul's comments in 2 Corinthians 12 verse by verse to see what is really being said.

2 Corinthians 12:2: *I know a man in Christ who fourteen years ago—whether in the body I do not know, or whether out of the body I do not know, God knows—such a one was caught up to the third heaven.*

2 Corinthians 12:3: *And I know such a man—whether in the body or out of the body I do not know, God knows—*

2 Corinthians 12:4: *how he was caught up into Paradise and heard inexpressible words, which it is not lawful for a man to utter.*

Paul is speaking of himself and his experience of being caught up into the third heaven. We know Paul is referring to himself because in verse 7, he declares that he was the one given a thorn in the flesh for the abundance of revelations. Paul wouldn't be given a thorn in the flesh for revelations given to someone else!

2 Corinthians 12:5: *Of such a one I will boast; yet of myself I will not boast, except in my infirmities.*

Paul's *"infirmities"* refer not to sicknesses but to his weaknesses, buffetings, and humiliation as an apostle who was persecuted throughout his ministry. We will see more of this in just a moment.

2 Corinthians 12:6: *For though I might desire to boast, I will not be a fool; for I will speak the truth. But I refrain, lest*

anyone should think of me above what he sees me to be or hears from me.

Paul's heart was to not be exalted due to his experience, but only to be received for the truth he shared and the man that he was.

2 Corinthians 12:7: *And lest I should be exalted above measure by the abundance of the revelations, a thorn in the flesh was given to me, a messenger of Satan to buffet me, lest I be exalted above measure.*

What is a thorn in the flesh?

The traditional explanation is that Paul had a chronic infirmity or perhaps an eye disease that God either gave him or refused to heal in order to keep Paul humble. This interpretation has destroyed the faith of multitudes of believers who need healing that Jesus provided on the cross.

Rather than a heart filled with faith and confidence in the redemptive right of healing, believers become double-minded and wavering, thinking that their sickness might be a thorn that God has chosen to not remove.

A THORN IN THE FLESH

Just what is a thorn in the flesh? When we let Scripture interpret Scripture, the answer is easy. Let's look at some examples in the Scriptures where similar language is used. Paul was certainly aware of these references and was comparing his experience to the following cases.

> *But if you do not drive out the inhabitants of the land from before you, then it shall be that those whom you let remain shall be irritants in your eyes and* **thorns in your sides***, and they shall harass you in the land where you dwell* (Numbers 33:55).

Israel was being exhorted by God to drive out the inhabitants of the Promised Land. If not, those who remained would become a problem to them. It would be hard to insert the traditional interpretation of sickness into this scenario. The irritants and thorns are people, enemy inhabitants in the land. This language is not describing a national sickness but rather the result of not expelling the enemy. The enemy would be a constant harassment to the peace of Israel.

> *Know for certain that the Lord your God will no longer drive out these nations from before you. But they shall be snares and traps to you, and scourges on your sides and* **thorns** *in your eyes, until you perish from this good land which the Lord your God has given you* (Joshua 23:13).

Is God speaking of a sickness that would affect all of Israel? No. It is figurative language that describes a persistent enemy that wasn't driven out of the land.

> *Therefore I also said, "I will not drive them out before you; but they shall be* **thorns in your side***, and their gods shall be a snare to you"* (Judges 2:3).

Again, the same. Thorn in the flesh is a saying that refers to a chronic or persistent enemy that hasn't been expelled from Israel's Promised land. When Paul used this language, he knew exactly what he was saying. There was a persistent enemy, a demon that harassed his ministry due to the abundance of his revelation. This enemy didn't come from God. It was a "messenger of Satan" sent to buffet him.

2 Corinthians 12:8-9: *Concerning this thing I pleaded with the Lord three times that it might depart from me. And He said to me, "My grace is sufficient for you, for My strength is made perfect in weakness." Therefore most gladly I will rather boast in my infirmities, that the power of Christ may rest upon me.*

Much like any of us, Paul got tired of dealing with a demonic presence that stirred up persecution and problems. Why didn't God respond favorably to Paul's request to remove the messenger of Satan?

The traditional interpretation has God saying, "Get over it, Paul, you can make it." But that isn't what is being said. Paul was asking for God to remove the enemy from his life—something that God never promised to do. Persecution was not nailed to the cross. Jesus bore our sins and sicknesses, but not persecution. God's response was that His grace—His unlimited provision and enablement—was sufficient. Paul was already equipped to handle the situation. But like many of us, he grew weary of the daily battle. He was inadvertently blaming God for the continued buffeting.

In essence, what God actually said to Paul is that "My sufficiency in all things is enough, Paul. You are equipped to deal with this. I have given you authority. My sufficiency and provision are more than enough in your time of need."

What is the grace that God speaks of? A great definition of grace can be found in the same letter of 2 Corinthians:

> *And God is able to make all grace abound toward you, **that you, always having all sufficiency in all things, may have an abundance for every good work*** (2 Corinthians 9:8).

"My grace is sufficient for you." Paul knew the answer and was already aware of God's grace. It was Paul who wrote of the armor of God and quenching all the fiery darts of the enemy. No doubt Paul was aware of what was penned by James: *"submit to God, resist the devil and he will flee"* (James 4:7). It wasn't that Paul was unequipped to be more than a conqueror. He was simply tired of having to conquer!

I doubt that many of us have a messenger of Satan assigned to us, and yet we grow weary and want God to make our problems disappear. The answer you need is the same answer that God gave to Paul—His grace! His abundant provision, strength, and enablement are more than sufficient to meet your need. You have the armor of God, the shield of faith, the name of Jesus, the Holy Spirit, the better covenant, the promises of God, the gifts of the Spirit, the mind of Christ, and the keys of the Kingdom at your disposal! You are equipped to win. His grace is sufficient. Don't blame your thorns on God. He has given you the resources of heaven in order to live victoriously on this earth!

Paul was not suffering from sickness. He was suffering the impact of a demonic messenger sent to make his life and ministry as tough as possible. Listen to how Paul described his ministry.

Are they ministers of Christ?—I speak as a fool—I am more: in labors more abundant, in stripes above measure, in prisons more frequently, in deaths often. From the Jews five times I received forty stripes minus one. Three times I was beaten with rods; once I was stoned; three times I was shipwrecked; a night and a day I have been in the deep; in journeys often, in perils of waters, in perils of robbers, in perils of my own countrymen, in perils of the Gentiles, in perils in the city, in perils in the wilderness, in perils in the sea, in perils among false brethren; in weariness and toil, in sleeplessness often, in hunger and thirst, in fastings often, in cold and nakedness—besides the other things, what comes upon me daily: my deep concern for all the churches (2 Corinthians 11:23-28).

It's interesting that in this list of sufferings and persecutions for the sake of the gospel, sickness is never mentioned! Sickness was not the thorn in the flesh. Sickness was not one of Paul's infirmities. Paul's thorn was the continual buffeting by the messenger of Satan who sought to humiliate Paul and make his progress as difficult as possible. God had called and equipped Paul to preach the gospel to the nations. This was a threat that the enemy sought to extinguish.

But what of Paul's remarks in the letter to the Galatians?

You know that because of physical infirmity I preached the gospel to you at the first. And my trial which was in my flesh you did not despise or reject, but you received me as an angel of God,

even as Christ Jesus. What then was the blessing
you enjoyed? For I bear you witness that, if possi-
ble, you would have plucked out your own eyes and
given them to me (Galatians 4:13-15).

It most certainly sounds like Paul was suffering in some
way in this passage. Paul's ministry to the Galatian region
occurred during his first missionary journey, which is
described in Acts 13 and 14. In this account of Paul's ministry and journey we can find no evidence of Paul being sick.
However there is one event that does give us a clue as to Paul's
sufferings:

Then Jews from Antioch and Iconium came there;
and having persuaded the multitudes, they stoned
Paul and dragged him out of the city, supposing
him to be dead. However, when the disciples gath-
ered around him, he rose up and went into the city.
And the next day he departed with Barnabas to
Derbe (Acts 14:19-20).

This took place in the region of Galatia. Paul was stoned
and left for dead, but God raised him up! From there he
departed to Derbe, a town in Galatia. Could it be that the letter to the Galatians is referring to this event and Paul's subsequent recovery from being stoned? I believe so. Perhaps the
rocks that struck his head and face caused swelling around
his eyes. Since we have no mention of Paul being sick during
this journey, I would suggest that the stoning was the affliction from which he had to fully recover.

Others who want to make a case for sickness will point to another verse in Galatians: *"See with what large letters I have written to you with my own hand!"* (Galatians 6:11).

Here, the argument is that Paul must have been suffering from an eye disease and was nearly blind. However, this does not hold up to closer scrutiny. The literal Greek rendering of this verse reads as follows: "See how 'great and quantitative' a 'writing' I have written to you with my own hand." Paul is simply referring to having written this epistle with his own hand. He did not dictate it to a scribe as was his custom.

When you understand Paul's story in the light of redemption, faith can rise in your heart and double-mindedness must leave!

Chapter 24

What About Job?

So many Christians seek understanding and comfort in the stories of Paul's thorn and Job. It is hard to fathom that Jesus and His victory over sin, sickness, death, and the devil is overlooked, while Job and Paul's thorn are embraced and misunderstood. This approach explains much of the reason for sickness in today's church.

The book of Job is not a manual for Christian living. The story of Job is not meant to be a pattern for the sons and daughter of God who are new creations walking in the promises of God! When reading Job, we need to understand some of the fundamental differences between Job and a New Covenant Christian believer.

To begin with, Job had no covenant with God. Job apparently lived before the time of Abraham and did not enjoy the kinds of promises that God had made to Abraham. For example, God had made a covenant with Abraham and that covenant included protection from his enemies.

After these things the word of the Lord came to Abram in a vision, saying, "Do not be afraid, Abram.

I am your shield, your exceedingly great reward"
(Genesis 15:1).

Similarly, we find the promises of God under the Law of Moses also protected Israel from their enemies.

The Lord will cause your enemies who rise against you to be defeated before your face; they shall come out against you one way and flee before you seven ways (Deuteronomy 28:7).

However, Job was exposed to his enemies and they quickly took or destroyed everything he had. There is no evidence of a covenant with God that established protection. As born-again believers, we have a better covenant established on better promises, and that covenant includes healing and protection!

He has obtained a more excellent ministry, inasmuch as He is also Mediator of a better covenant, which was established on better promises (Hebrews 8:6).

Job also had no knowledge of the devil. He was not aware that the devil was the *"god of this world"* (2 Corinthians 4:4 KJV), *"the prince of the power of the air"* (Ephesians 2:2), the *"thief"* (John 10:10), and that the whole world was under his rule (1 John 5:19, Luke 4:5-6). Job had very limited knowledge and assumed that his troubles came from God. He even accused God of afflicting him on various occasions.

For the arrows of the Almighty are within me; my spirit drinks in their poison; the terrors of God are arrayed against me (Job 6:4).

This does not sound like a man who knew his God and walked in covenant with Him! Even God rebuked Job when He finally appeared to him.

Then the Lord answered Job out of the whirlwind, and said: "Who is this who darkens counsel by words without knowledge?" (Job 38:1-2)

Now we know so much more under the New Covenant. We know that our fight isn't with God but with *"principalities"* and *"powers,"* and that we have been given faith in order to quench all the *"fiery darts of the wicked one"* (Ephesians 6:12-16).

Job had a very limited knowledge of God. He himself confessed his ignorance at the end of the book:

I have heard of You by the hearing of the ear, but now my eye sees You. Therefore I abhor myself, and repent in dust and ashes (Job 42:5-6).

A few verses earlier Job had declared his own ignorance:

…Therefore I have uttered what I did not understand, things too wonderful for me, which I did not know (Job 42:3).

Job was a man with limited knowledge. He had limited knowledge of God and no knowledge of Satan. Under the New Covenant we have the maximum revelation of God, greater than the revelation of Abraham, greater than Moses and the Law. We have Jesus, God in the flesh. And we see the will of God revealed fully in Jesus when He went about doing good and healing all who were oppressed of the devil because God was with Him (Acts 10:38).

JOB'S LIMITATIONS

One of the most important differences between Job and a New Covenant believer is that the believer is a new creation, born again by the Spirit of God! Job was not born again, nor was anyone in the Bible before the resurrection of Jesus. Thus, they were limited to their sin nature and sensory knowledge. God could not relate to Old Testament saints as He can relate to us. We are His workmanship, created in Christ Jesus (Ephesians 2:10). Job was a natural man with no covenant and limited knowledge.

Job also had no weapons with which to fight the enemy. Since he had no covenant, he was defenseless. However, we have been given the name of Jesus, the power of the blood, the filling of the Holy Spirit, the precious promises of God, the armor of God, the gifts of the Spirit, the keys of the Kingdom, the Word of God, the power of faith that can move mountains, the Spirit of power, love, and a sound mind, and we have been blessed with all blessings! We are well-equipped to overcome the enemy and any sickness or destructive work that he may attempt to put on us.

Job lived in fear. Fear is the natural state of fallen mankind. Faith was turned into fear when Adam and Eve sinned. Job worshipped in fear since he really didn't know who he was worshipping.

*For the thing I greatly feared has come upon me,
and what I dreaded has happened to me. I am not
at ease, nor am I quiet; I have no rest, for trouble
comes* (Job 3:25-26).

This is not the confidence of a man who knows God and is standing in faith in a covenant!

Finally, Job didn't have an intercessor. The devil had access to God through Adam's sin. He could accuse men and women day and night, and thus he did with Job. However, Jesus has defeated sin, the devil, and death and has sat down at the right hand of God and ever lives to make intercession for us.

*Therefore He is also able to save to the uttermost those
who come to God through Him, since He always lives
to make intercession for them* (Hebrews 7:25).

Job was blessed by God because he was a man of integrity in spite of his limited knowledge, but he was not protected with a covenant. The accuser had full access to Job. It could appear that God was giving the devil permission to attack Job because of his accusations, but we see in the book of James, that God cannot be tempted with evil nor does He tempt anyone.

*Let no one say when he is tempted, "I am tempted
by God"; for God cannot be tempted by evil, nor
does He Himself tempt anyone* (James 1:13).

Whatever we see happening in the book of Job between God and the devil, we know based on the revelation in James that the devil was not successfully provoking God to test Job or tempt him with evil. Satan was the god of this world from the moment that Adam sinned, and he had full access to Job. God was blessing Job, but because there was no covenant and limited faith in Job's life, the enemy could wreak havoc. God's blessing on Job's life probably gave the devil pause, but God didn't allow anything in Job's life that wasn't already unleashed through Adam's sin.

> *The righteousness of the upright will deliver them...* (Proverbs 11:6).

Though Job was a fearful man and accused God for his troubles, in his limited knowledge he held on to his integrity. There was no Law that convicted him of sin, so in that sense he was righteous. There was only an enemy that wanted to destroy him.

JOB IS NOT OUR EXAMPLE

Job is not an example for our Christian experience, nor an example of the covenant we have by the blood of Jesus. Our covenant includes healing. Job said, *"The Lord gave, and the Lord has taken away"* (Job 1:21). But God didn't say that. Jesus said, *"The thief does not come except to steal, and to kill, and to destroy. I have come that they may have life, and that they may have it more abundantly!"* (John 10:10). Unfortunately, many choose Job's words of ignorance over Jesus' words of revelation.

Job's story is not indicative of God's dealings with us under the New Covenant. They are not comparable in any way. Job lived with the most limited understanding of God. All true understanding must begin with Jesus, not Job. Job's sufferings reveal the power of ignorance and fear to allow suffering and loss. Many Christians allow suffering and fear in their lives because they do not know the true nature of God and the power of His covenant.

Satan is a defeated foe and we have been given authority over him. We are to resist him, and he will flee.

> *Submit yourselves therefore to God. Resist the devil, and he will flee from you* (James 4:7 KJV).

Satan no longer has access to God in order to accuse us. Jesus is our Advocate and Intercessor. Rather than identify with and draw comfort from Job in your affliction, why not look to Jesus who died to give you the victory? We must look to Jesus for deliverance, authority, faith, and healing!

Nothing of human suffering—other than persecution for our faith—was left off the cross. Jesus took all sin, sickness, and suffering on Himself and then gave the church authority over all of it. The problems in the world aren't from God. The problem is that the church has been taught that we are simple pawns and God is orchestrating our suffering for some mysterious reason. This is the greatest lie ever perpetrated by the enemy and it is another reason why there is so much sickness in the body of Christ.

Chapter 25

There Is
Grace for You

I end this book where I began—by speaking of the grace of God. While the information I have presented is meant to enlighten, bring freedom, and inspire faith in God's goodness, I don't want this to be a five-step program for healing. I don't want believers to feel guilty that their condition may be a result of their lifestyles. Obviously, knowledge is better than ignorance and anything we can know and do to walk in good health is a good thing. Regardless of the immediate source of sickness, the original source was Adam's sin, and Jesus has taken that curse upon Himself. We receive healing because of what He did, not because of what we do. Once we can understand and cooperate with the "finished work of the cross," healing will come.

The greatest need is to believe that God cares about you and that God has made provision for health and healing. As long as we believe we have to earn a healing or that God may be using sickness in our lives for some mysterious reason, we will remain limited in the area of faith. Faith can only respond to the degree that there is certainty in God's goodness.

Some are suffering and don't know why. They feel they have done everything they know to do, and they remain sick. Some have lost hope or have concluded that all that has been shared in this book can't be true.

Please permit me to share a few more truths with you that perhaps will bring hope and faith to your heart.

For the grace of God that brings salvation has appeared to all men (Titus 2:11).

Salvation is a big subject and includes every aspect of mankind's suffering and need. Sin unleashed the power of death, sickness and loss. It is God's grace that brings salvation, and it is available to all people.

The word "salvation" in Titus 2:11 is the word *soterion,* and it means salvation, health, and deliverance. Let's reread the verse with those words inserted: For the grace of God has appeared that offers salvation, health, and deliverance to all people.

It is good to know that grace has made a way! Grace is available to all! In fact, we could define grace as God's exceedingly abundant provision for our every need. No need that you have was left off the cross. All was covered and there is grace for every need in your life. There is grace for your healing and health. There is no lack.

Jesus commissioned the disciples to take His grace to the people, saying, *"Heal the sick, cleanse the lepers, raise the dead, cast out demons. Freely you have received, freely give"* (Matthew 10:8). The word "freely" refers to God's grace: *"...But where sin abounded, grace abounded much more"* (Romans 5:20).

When you understand that Adam's sin is the root and sickness is a fruit, you can easily substitute the word "sickness" for "sin" and gain a deeper understanding: But where sickness abounded, grace abounded much more!

The point is that there is no human need that falls outside of God's grace. He has provided for every sickness and affliction. If we could simply believe in His goodness and understand His purpose, it should be easy to receive from Him. If the woman with the issue of blood could receive healing because she believed that He was that good, you can too!

Once you have a revelation of His goodness and provision, your faith will come alive.

> *When she heard about Jesus, she came behind Him in the crowd and touched His garment. For she said, "If only I may touch His clothes, I shall be made well"* (Mark 5:27-28).

FAITH RECEIVES HEALING

Faith doesn't create a healing. Faith receives the healing that already exists by grace.

It is time to look at all of the revelations of God's love that speak of healing. The power of His name, His blood, His Spirit, His promises, His covenant, His gifts, His faith, and the keys to His Kingdom are His grace for you!

He who did not spare His own Son, but delivered
Him up for us all, how shall He not with Him also
freely give us all things? (Romans 8:32)

Do you believe that God's goodness is enough to heal you? The multitudes who sought out Jesus weren't giants of faith or Bible college graduates. They simply believed in His goodness. They believed there was grace for their need.

What is your need for grace compared to the sacrifice of Jesus for humanity? Our needs pale in comparison. If God did not spare His Son, how can we believe for one moment that healing is in a different class? Jesus *is* the Healer! If Jesus was delivered up for us all, healing is included in the deal!

Can you freely receive what has been freely given? Is there any reason why you can't receive what grace has already provided?

Through whom also we have access by faith into
this grace in which we stand... (Romans 5:2).

The grace you need is available through faith. In other words, the free gift is received by believing that the Giver wants you to have it. God is a Giver.

Every good gift and every perfect gift is from above,
and comes down from the Father of lights, with
whom there is no variation or shadow of turning
(James 1:17).

Why would multitudes follow Jesus into the wilderness for healing if they thought He was going to point out their sin, embarrass them, and explain why sickness was for their benefit? Nobody would search out Jesus if He did that. The love of God simply flowed from Him. He is always "yes" and "amen" (2 Corinthians 1:20). People followed Jesus because He was good. He healed them all.

Get your hopes up! It is never too late. It is never too hard. Healing is always God's will. There is grace for you today!

Do not fear, little flock, for it is your Father's good pleasure to give you the kingdom (Luke 12:32).

> *Father, I pray that those who need healing would see Your goodness and receive your grace of healing. You have sent Your Word to heal us, and we receive that Word now in the powerful name of Jesus! Amen!*

About the Author

A graduate of Christ for the Nations Institute in Dallas, Texas, Barry Bennett has served the Lord since 1972. He and his wife, Betty Kay, ministered to Cambodian refugees in Dallas for nearly three years and served as missionaries in Mexico, Guatemala, and Chile for more than twelve years.

In 2001, they returned to Texas where Barry served as director and teacher at a Spanish language Bible institute. In 2007, Barry joined Andrew Wommack Ministries.

Today, Barry serves as the Dean of Instructors and is an instructor at Charis Bible College in Woodland Park, Colorado, where he's passionate about teaching the practical truths of God's Word. Barry and Betty Kay have three children and six grandchildren.

Visit Barry at
www.barrybennett.org

and on Facebook at
www.facebook.com/officialbarrybennett/

OUR VISION

Proclaiming the truth and the power of the Gospel of Jesus Christ with excellence. Challenging Christians to live victoriously, grow spiritually, know God intimately.

Connect with us on

Facebook @ **HarrisonHousePublishers**

and Instagram @ **HarrisonHousePublishing**

so you can stay up to date with news about our books and our authors.

Visit us at **www.harrisonhouse.com**

for a complete product listing as well as monthly specials for wholesale distribution.